First Printing: 2020

ISBN 978-1-913218-90-4

Printed in Great Britain by
Biddles Books Limited, King's Lynn, Norfolk

SECRETS OF
Transylvania

DIANA POP COMSA

Photographs Gabriel Motica

Foreword Aura Woodward

To my grandmother

About the Team

DIANA POP COMSA was born and raised in Transylvania where she spent a happy childhood between her hometown of Baia Mare and her grandparents dairy farms in the Apuseni Mountains and in Maramures. Her academic and professional life has subsequently led her to Bucharest, Vienna, Nice, Paris, San Francisco and London.

In an age where luxury is being redefined by time well spent, protecting heritage, and producing in more sustainable ways, Diana believes that we have a unique opportunity in not letting the last remaining generations of artisans and age old rural practices disappear forever in the face of mass production and younger people turning to different lifestyles.

Traditional crafts can be the bridge between the past and the future, and by supporting them we can ensure the continuity of entire communities. The author hopes to impart to her daughters and the wider public the beauty of rural Transylvanian life and landscape and inspire them to explore this region.

A graduate of EDHEC business school in France, Diana is a marketing and big data specialist working for luxury retail and media groups like LVMH and Conde Nast.

A passion for nature in general and mountains in particular has led GABRIEL MOTICA to take up the art of photography, aiming to capture the beauty of the world around him. Over thirty years later, photography is still the leading force behind his stories, travels, and the people he meets.

Gabriel finds himself time and time again aiming his lens to the rural traditions and celebrations of Transylvania. He is a passionate supporter of raising awareness for the region and helping perpetuate the skills of the artisans he meets.

Gabriel is a graduate of the School of Photographic Arts and Cinematography from Baia Mare and a member of the Romanian Association of Photographic Artists. He has held several exhibitions and launched books that showcase the beauty of Northern Transylvania and Maramures, regions for which he is also a tourism ambassador.

Transylvanian born, AURA WOODWARD is a charity executive and communication professional. Over the last 15 years she has served The Prince of Wales's Charities. More recently she was the Executive Director of The Prince of Wales's Foundation Romania, a charity which supports heritage preservation and rural development. Aura

is passionate about creating opportunities for local communities through education and training. While working for The Prince of Wales she developed in Romania a number of programmes to support the preservation of local medieval architecture and small independent farmers.

Prior to this she was a journalist for the BBC World Service covering extensively the EU accession negotiations and judicial reforms of the former communist countries in Eastern Europe.

Aura is educated in law and journalism and has recently completed the Executive Leadership Programme at Oxford University. She lives in England with her husband and their two sons.

Table of Contents

Foreword

It's a bear!

It was a beautiful sunny morning in Transylvania with a perfect blue sky. I was commuting from the medieval town of Sighisoara to Viscri, a small village nestled between gentle hills. I loved travelling through this magical landscape, where nature unfolded in all its glory. It wasn't unusual to come across rare birds or wild animals, during my travels. That morning it was a brown bear, running unabated alongside the main road.

Romania has nearly half of all brown bears in Europe, which amounts to about six thousand bears. They live alongside wildcats, red deer or wolves in the Carpathian Mountains, the last wilderness in Europe. The last eight kilometres to Viscri are through poor country roads which force you to slow down. But you are rewarded with enormous canvases of nature painted with the most rare and beautiful flowers, which disappeared from the rest of Europe.

And in the middle of this extraordinary natural habitat are small towns and villages settled many hundreds of years ago. You will be alerted by the spires of churches; at least two or three in every village, however small. The communities who live in those settlements are just as diverse as the landscape around them. For centuries, Romanians, Hungarians, Germans (or Saxons as the locals call them), Roma, and other minorities built communities together while worshiping in multiple languages in Orthodox, Catholic, Protestant or Unitarian churches.

I am a charity worker and I've spent the last fifteen years working to preserve Transylvania's architectural heritage. From the historic Maramures in the north with its exquisite wooden buildings and Rosia Montana in the west with its Roman gold mines to the medieval settlements in the south of Transylvania,

I've met remarkable crafts people, listened to their stories and learnt so much from this mythical land.

My commute that morning came to an end as I approached Viscri. Its fortified church from the 1300s waves to you from the distance. The houses have facades vividly painted by local crafts people while the only road in the village is flooded with geese, hens and dogs. The Cows' Parade is the real attraction. It happens every evening when cows, horses, donkeys and sheep return home from the nearby pastures. English travellers, in particular, are amazed to see that Transylvanian cows do actually return home and wait patiently outside the gate for their owners to let them in.

There are about 250 medieval villages like Viscri in southern Transylvania, albeit not all are in the same good shape. These traditional settlements were built from 1100 onwards by Germanic settlers, many of whom moved to Germany after the collapse of communism. It is now down to the new communities and the many charities to preserve the local architecture.

Despite the changes in the communities, the way of life here has barely changed for centuries. The way people look after their land and procure their food, the way they interact with nature and its unwritten rules, the way they respect each other's traditions and faiths are largely untouched.

Food is just about celebrating life as it is about nourishing. The most popular dishes are those which can be shared with your family and friends, and sometimes with strangers too. The food in the countryside is largely home grown and organic, although not certified as such. The old recipes may get a twist with a few flakes of fresh truffles, chanterelles mushrooms picked from the nearby hills or perhaps with some organic honey which you can find in abundance.

This magical land, with its troubled history, continues to inspire and fascinate artists, writers and travellers alike. Our mission is to find that right balance between the unstoppable development and the need to preserve its authentic charm.

Aura Woodward

Introduction

WELCOME to my own, private Transylvania, deep in the heart of central Romania, on the southeastern edge of Europe! It is one hundred thousand square kilometres of idyllic, almost untouched countryside and home to over six million people, including my family.

Transylvania is the keeper of all the sights, sounds and tastes of my childhood, and despite the passage of time, cruel communism and a bloody revolution, all my magical memories still exist in this mysterious land. All one has to do to experience the real, untouched Transylvania is slow down and poke around in all its remote corners, into the places where no mobile phone coverage or WiFi can reach and listen to the 'time stands still' stories of the village elders.

Transylvania is portrayed as the land of bloodthirsty vampires and howling wolves. Well, the wolves are certainly there, but sadly Dracula himself is only the stuff of legends. Nevertheless, there are plenty of equally fascinating stories in this virtually undiscovered corner of Europe.

In this book I do not go deeply into the region's rich and complex history. Nor is this an exhaustive travel directory. Instead I am taking you on a tour of village life and values, learned during my time spent in the Apuseni Mountains and National Park, and also in beautiful Maramures County, which boasts a grand total of eight UNESCO heritage sites! My parents and relatives still live in these areas and it's where I regularly return to visit.

The first five years of my life were spent on my maternal grandparents' farm in the Apuseni Mountains, a self-sufficient holding with roaming dairy cattle, fruit orchards and vegetable patches. In the '80s, many children lived with the grandparents while their parents had been allocated jobs by the Communist Government upon graduating university, often far away from their city of choice. City shops also experienced shortages across many product categories and farms were regarded as a more dependable environment to raise young children. Our farm had an outdoor oven for baking heavenly-smelling bread and cakes, and endless wild gardens for myself and the neighbours' children to romp in.

When school beckoned it was time to permanently join my parents in the city. However, I didn't lose touch with my own little piece of paradise. I went back to this village for four months every year, during school holidays, until I was sixteen. Each time I would pick up where I left off, finding the same friends, places and activities of the season.

This mountain village is called Manastireni and it was first mentioned in historical documents in 1332 in the register of papal dues. It is also the only place in northern Transylvania appearing in the family tree of the last seven generations of the British royal family! The Kemeny's were the most important noble family linked to Manastireni. As a thank you for their pro-Hapsburg support, the title of Baron of Manastireni was bestowed on them by Austrian emperor Leopold I. One of the members of the Kemeny family, Cristina Kemeny, is the great-great-great-great-great grandmother of Queen Elizabeth II.

The other village which was important in my formative years was Durusa, in Maramures County, where my Dad was born, and where we spent most weekends. This earth, these traditions, these values, raised me, and a piece of my heart is always firmly embedded in Transylvania wherever I roam on this planet.

There is a tidal rift between life in the cities and life in the villages. The cities are vibrant and modernising fast following the austerity of the Ceausescu regime, which we hardly felt the impact of deep in the self-sufficient countryside, or perhaps I just don't remember. The cities attract more tourists, especially the capital of Transylvania, Cluj but also Sibiu, Brasov, and Sighisoara are popular destinations. However, this book shines a light on the region's villages, their timeless traditions and beauty. I hope you will see my work as an open invitation to wander beyond your comfort zone; to discover different sights and be inspired by alternative lifestyles. Many people are fascinated by the beauty of Transylvania's villages. HRH Prince Charles is a devotee of the region and lauds the rural customs and eco-friendly practices whenever he visits. He has commissioned numerous artists to capture its rich flora and has restored rural property in Viscri in the southeastern corner.

This little slice of Romania is finding itself on more and more lists of 'best places to visit', featuring in the shortlists of various prestigious travel magazines, and even on international catwalks, its textiles, textures and colours inspiring famous designers.

From my family to yours, THIS is my secret Transylvania. Happy discovering!

Nature Or The World As I Know It

WHEN I THINK of Transylvania, its landscape is what comes to mind first: mountains, hills, forests, rivers, meadows, the sound of crickets and birds calling. The image is so vivid I can almost feel the breeze, smell the freshly cut grass, and hear the sounds of a busy village. Romania is only six per cent of the total territory of the EU but home to a third of all its farms. The vast majority are small family holdings. In my memory everywhere was always bursting with life - flowers, birds, insects - fluffy, white clouds scattered across the deep blue sky, and horses and people toiling in the fields. That is a regular day in Transylvania.

The village communities have always had a deep respect for nature with their entire livelihoods revolving around each season and the produce. My grandparents, like their ancestors before them used methods not seen in the rest of Europe for more than a century. The perpetuation of these traditions is fuelled by elders wanting life to remain the same, but also by limited financial means to automate small-scale subsistence farming.

As children we were always told to 'work with what you have', 'learn not to depend on others', 'do what you need to do and do it well'. My Grandpa's favourite sayings are loosely translated by 'don't leave for tomorrow what you can do today' and 'lay your bed well if you want a good sleep'.

Due to Transylvania's strategic position at the crossroads of empires in the east and in the west, migrant invasions have often sent residents fleeing to the Carpathian Mountains, and to the forests encircling the Transylvanian plains. Nature never failed to protect the fugitives, giving them plenty of shelter, food and raw materials. These mountains are a natural fortress. WWF refer to the Southern Carpathians as the last intact forest landscape in continental Europe.

There are caves and peaks that can only be reached on foot, or on horseback. However, in times of peace, the farmers have gone about their work in the fields, following the rules passed down to them through the generations.

A local saying goes: 'Romanians are brothers with the forest' because of their affinity with the protective woods. Even the name Transylvania comes from the Latin words 'trans' and 'silva' meaning 'over the forest'. When I was young, the forests were not without dangers. They still are home to Europe's largest brown bear population, and lynx and numerous wolf packs are easily found. Recent years have seen the reintroduction of the European bison on a reservation in the south of Transylvania near the village of Armenis. Foreign tourists come on animal watching holidays. We watched for them too, but ready to run, rather than take pictures. The reason these animals have survived in such large numbers to this day is lack of contact with humans, despite hunting being practiced. However, farmers only kill what they need to protect their livelihoods.

The hills and mountains also hold the lure of natural treasures like gold, silver, iron, copper, salt, marble, as well as coal and uranium among others. Did you know that the largest gold reserves in Europe are in Transylvania in a region called Rosia Montana? There are also vast amounts of silver here. When a Canadian mining corporation sought to obtain a permit to open a mine, it marked the first major commitment of civil society since the fall of communism to protect the landscape and villages of this area and not have it lost forever in the face of exploitation and heavy mining.

Living away from the region and experiencing bigger and bustling cities like Paris, San Francisco or London has only made me appreciate nature more. It is a palette far richer than anything man could design. Botanists, like UK's John Akeroyd, rave about Transylvania's lowland wildflower meadows, 'which are of a sort that have virtually disappeared in Europe'. A notable mention goes to the ADEPT Foundation and their efforts in the past fifteen years to influence policy and help preserve the landscape and farming communities. The team has hands-on experience with thousands of villagers in the southeastern corner of Transylvania and are relentless at finding innovative ways to protect this unique environment.

Fay Ballard, daughter of the late novelist JG Ballard, said: ' These meadows are of world significance…Some of the watercolours by local and visiting artists document plants that grow nowhere else or in few other places. You can walk through these pastures of high wildflowers. It's just heaven.' Some of the wildflowers I loved growing up were campanula and crocus with their fresh, delicate scent, sweet gentian and peppery geraniums, hepatica or hellebore. Wild daffodils were incredibly fragrant in spring and we used to spend Sunday afternoons picking them from forest clearings.

Transylvania is rich in so many ways. But the challenges of globalisation and climate change are taking a toll. Natural disasters like landslides and floods have destroyed entire areas, not enough trees are being planted making the ecosystem very fragile. There needs to be a wider market for local produce if the villagers are to maintain their lifestyle. I hope that more efforts will be made to protect the variety and richness of the environment so future generations can enjoy this unique beauty.

Historical Highlights

AT THE CROSSROADS of empires and in the path of numerous migrant invasions, Transylvania was always destined to have a complex story. Today's population of 6.7 million is an ethnic stew of Romanian, Hungarian, German, Slavic and Roma people, plus a few extra stragglers who have seeped across the border over the centuries. Eighty percent of those who live here are ethnic Romanian, and another sixteen percent Hungarian, but even the minor nationalities have left their mark on this vibrant region.

A group of tribesmen called Thracians were the first people to be mentioned in the area, with a history dating back 3000 years and speaking an Indo-European language. The Dacians, who lived on the land that covers today's Romania, and therefore all of Transylvania, were Thracian people. Dacia was conquered in 106 AD by the Roman Empire, its rich natural resources were an irresistible draw for Emperor Trajan, or Marcus Ulpius Traianus.

The Romans colonised Dacia for 170 years and left their ubiquitous stamp on the language, the culture, and the people. The origin of the Romanian language dates back to the Roman conquest of Dacia. During that time, colloquial Latin used by soldiers, clerks and other people coming from different parts of the Roman Empire mixed with a minority of local Thracian / Dacian words giving birth to a neo-Latin language that lives on to this day, Romanian.

In the centuries that followed various Barbarian invasions crossed this land – from the Mongols, Goths, Visigoths, Slaves, Tatars, to the Huns. The latter, descendants of the people once led by Attila the Hun, started attacking Dacia around 900 AD. They were a nomadic tribe originally from the Ural Mountains in Asia, who had settled on the Pannonian Plains in what is today's Hungary. The Huns were a ferocious, warring people and their attacks and conquests in Transylvania spanned almost 400 years, before it became a province of the Kingdom of Hungary, ruled by Hungarian princes.

From 1541 when the Kingdom of Hungary dissolved and until 1688, the Principality of Transylvania was an autonomous state, the local Romanian population still ruled by Hungarian princes, but at the same time also a vassal to the Ottoman Empire.

One of the greatest national heroes is Michael the Brave, ruler of Wallachia, today's southern Romania. He took on the Ottoman Empire, actively fighting them for several years before becoming the de facto ruler of Transylvania in 1599. He became the Imperial Governor of Transylvania and cemented his rule by invading Moldavia in the east and becoming the Prince of this third region as well. He managed to hang onto power for less than a year before he was assassinated. This union, albeit short lived, was the first time Romanians from all three main provinces of Transylvania, Wallachia and Moldavia were united under the same ruler.

Transylvania should also be remembered as the first place in Europe where religious tolerance was proclaimed. The foreign rulers granted the right to join Unitarianism, a Christian movement that believed God to be one person, as opposed to the Trinity of the Father, the Son and the Holy Spirit. The openness for this religion in Transylvania was in direct contrast to what was happening across the rest of Europe at that time, where any deviation from the Catholic beliefs was deemed heresy and was heavily punished.

The Turda proclamation read: 'no one shall be reviled for his religion by anyone . . . and it is not permitted that anyone should threaten anyone else by imprisonment. . . . For faith is the gift of God. . . .' However, Unitarianism had a majority Hungarian following which meant that the majority of Transylvanians who were Orthodox did not benefit from this proclamation. The Orthodox religion was still not officially recognised.

HUNGARY

SATU MARE

MARAMUREȘ

BISTRIȚ.
NĂSĂU

SĂLAJ

BIHOR

CLUJ

MURE

T R A N S Y L V A N

ARAD

ALBA

SIBIU

TIMIȘ

HUNEDOARA

R O M

VÂLCEA

A

GORJ

CARAȘ-
SEVERIN

Belgrade

★

SERBIA

MEHEDINȚI

OLT

DOLJ

LEGEND:

Greater Transylvania today, shown here
within Romania's administrative county lines.

0   100 miles

0   100 km

From 1690, Transylvania became part of the Austro-Hungarian Empire and was under the control of the Ottomans and the Habsburgs. They declared the local Romanian speaking population not fit to govern and proclaimed the Hungarian, Saxons and Szekelys as the only ruling nations for all official positions in Transylvania. The Romanian speaking farmers suffered hugely, could not own property and had to pay fees. The rulers also pressured Orthodox leaders to join the Catholic Church.

The native Romanians fought for hundreds of years against the injustice and oppression, trying to re-establish their rightful identity, but in vain. In 1848 as the Hungarian revolution was taking shape, plans were drawn up to absorb Transylvania into Hungary proper. There was talk of emancipating the Transylvanian serfs but with no official recognition of the Romanian language and no representation of the Romanian speaking population in any legislative and executive bodies. The Saxon rulers objected, fearing loss of their privilege so they joined Transylvanians and other Romanians in a civil war against the Hungarians. The Habsburgs supported the Transylvanians and eventually Transylvanians were finally recognised as a separate nation alongside their Orthodox religion, and farmers were given land, but barely enough to survive. The dual monarchy Austria - Hungary was born, ruled by Emperor Franz Josef. It would last until World War I.

Going through the paperwork from my Dad's childhood home led to some interesting findings. The contracts and doctor's notes dating back to the late 19th century are all in Hungarian and some stamps even feature Emperor's Franz Josef face. My great grandfather said that the local notary public used a translator if the parties were not fluent in Hungarian.

After World War I, the Austro-Hungarian Empire dismantled, Transylvania united with Romania, which already comprised the Romanian speaking principalities of Wallachia and Moldova. The new, united country was called Romania Mare or 'Great Romania', and the border included almost all historical Romanian land. The 1920s and 1930s were a tumultuous period of corruption, political manoeuvring and the rise of fascism both locally and regionally in the Balkans. The rise of the ultra-nationalistic and anti-Semitic 'Iron Guard' in Romania coincided with the crowning of Prince Michael. He became king in

1927, aged only six years old, after his grandfather's death, and following his father's self-imposed exile.

When a regency council failed to govern the country correctly, King Mihai's father returned to rule his country in 1930, until Mihai became king again in 1940. He was still only 19. At the same time, General Ion Antonescu, a military dictator, took power becoming Prime Minister. He brought the 'Iron Guard', a fascist movement and party, into the heart of his government.

When Romania was again forced to cede much of northern Transylvania to Hungary during the Second World War, Antonescu allied himself with the Nazis and sent troops to fight Russia's Red Army. They also carried out pogroms and political assassinations, including the horrific slaying of Romanian Jews and Roma people, including children, at a slaughterhouse in the capital Bucharest.

In 1944 King Michael overthrew his Prime Minister. He had Antonescu arrested then joined the Allies in the fight against Germany. But a year later political pressure saw a pro-Soviet communist government installed. King Michael was forced to abdicate in 1947. He had left the country to attend the wedding of his cousins, Queen Elizabeth II and Prince Philip.

A Soviet-influenced People's Republic was formed, which centralised everything and gave full authority to the Communist Party. Governmental institutions served merely as the machinery to carry out party decisions. This included forced collectivisation of agriculture, the dissolving of private organizations and the curtailed activities of churches. In their place, and mainly in order to mobilise public opinion, the communists created mass organisations in every walk of life.

In 1965, Nicolae Ceausescu became the General Secretary of the Communist Party and imposed one of the most repressive rules. His mismanagement of Romania crippled the country. He exported vast amounts of agricultural and industrial products in a drive to eradicate all foreign debt which was achieved in the spring of 1989.

This ambition created massive shortages at home and severe rationing had to be implemented throughout the 1980s. Dissent against Ceausescu was rife and the popular uprising of December 1989, which eventually led to his death in the middle of a bloody revolution, started in Timisoara. One of the most famous anti-communist voices in the 1980s came from Cluj, the unofficial capital of Transylvania. Doina Cornea, a professor at Babes Bolyai University, had repeatedly put her own life in danger to protest against the government.

People could now elect their own president but this newly found democracy also spurred a tumultuous political period. Several loans from the World Bank and the International Monetary Fund did not solve the problem of poverty or bring sustained economic growth. Austere economic reforms led to unrest and riots which continued throughout the 1990s. By the Millenium, the focus was on perceived stability and European Union accession. Romania joined the EU in 2007, notwithstanding numerous warnings about the level of corruption in the country. Anger against that corruption has simmered throughout the first two decades of this century. The largest anti-corruption demonstrations since communism fell took place in 2017, when more than 200,000 people took to the streets across the country.

The difficult road to independence has shaped the national characteristics of the people, who are very resilient and supremely adaptable to change. A well-known poem 'The Third Letter' by acclaimed Romanian author Mihai Eminescu describes perfectly the mentality of the Romanian people: 'We will happily carry all burdens, in times of peace or in times of war'.

Transylvania is a rich canvas of languages, cultures, religions and ethnicities. Nowadays students at Babes Bolyai University in Cluj can study for their degree in Romanian, German, Hungarian, English or French. My parents completed their studies in Romanian, but I have friends who studied in French or German. Street signs in some larger cities can be in Hungarian or German as well as Romanian.

As a witness to just a small slice of this incredibly rich history, I fervently hope the path to future change and reform will become smoother than it has been in the past. Now, I so wish to see Transylvania, and indeed all of Romania, with its amazing natural resources and people, flourish economically and socially.

Homemade Heaven

Travel to Transylvania today and you could easily feel that you have wandered into a postcard from another era. Villagers still go about their daily work in much the same way as their parents and grandparents did before them.

I never gave much thought to our back garden when I was a child. Well, that is not entirely true. In fact, I employed every tactic I could to avoid working there, it wasn't a place for fun and games. Weeding, digging, picking, sorting, and washing vegetables was all anyone did in that back garden; hard labour in my opinion.

I wasn't work-shy but my favourite activity was haymaking. This meant a hike across the hills to get to our family fields, or a journey in the horse-drawn cart if we had to go very far. Grandpa would always let me hold the reins and guide the horses. After lunch we would take a short nap together under a tree, followed by a bit more work, then a fun journey back home, alongside many other families. It was a real community activity and I loved everything about it.

Looking after the back garden had none of that thrill, but it was what fed us. Grandma was religious about the vegetable patch, nurturing an abundant array of plants to make sure we had a little bit of everything that was in season to eat. She grew potatoes, turnips, onions, carrots, parsley, green beans, tomatoes and cabbages, as well as various herbs for cooking, or to use as natural remedies.

It was a fairly large piece of flat land, behind the house, conveniently nestled between the barn and a small stream, and at the foot of a hill. This meant it was protected from the wind, didn't need watering, and there was plenty of manure from the family's horses and cows ready to use as natural compost every spring and autumn.

Fruit trees surrounded the vegetable garden. Wonderful bushes covered with everything from gooseberries to red and black currants, blackberries and raspberries. I lost count of how many injuries I incurred over the years, trying to get to our neighbour's slightly better tasting gooseberries on the other side of those bushes. We had an abundance of apple trees and a few pear and walnut trees, stretching all the way up the hill. These gardens were self-perpetuating. Seeds were kept from one year to the next, or traded with other families in the village, in a quest for a better harvest the following season.

The view from the top of that hill is still my favourite to this day. A delicate stream runs all along the base of the hill across several gardens, and from the top I could listen to the hubbub of the bustling village below. I would sit up there endlessly and try to identify the various sounds. Who was chopping wood? Whose horses were trotting? Who was a loud greeter? Whose dog was angry? Which church bells were tolling among the three churches in the village? The crickets would be chirping all around me and it was my happy place for so many years, and still is really.

The farmers of Manastireni have always been, like the communities in all villages, very self-sufficient. As well as growing their own food, the garden is also home to natural remedies. Stomach pains went away with warmed up green cabbage leaves applied directly to the stomach, garden sorrel tea was a remedy for stomach flu. Horseradish root wrapped in a cloth, then applied to the forehead, was efficient against headaches or toothaches. Vinegar and garlic massaged against the forehead sent headaches away, however not a remedy I would rush to use. A baked, and peeled onion is great for coughs, or you can use yarrow tea. All these secrets were passed from one generation to the next, and people would use them religiously, long before pharmacies appeared on every street corner in nearby towns.

In such a prolific environment the cellar of Grandpa and Grandma's house was invaluable. A bit dank and scary for a small child like me, but deliciously cool during the hot summer months, and where we kept all the vegetables and fruit necessary to sustain us over winter. Apples and potatoes were stored there, as well as all the preserves and pickles Grandma had laboured over.

We also used the space in the attic near the chimney to hang and smoke home-made pork sausages and the Romanian delicacy, *slanina*, which is basically sections of pork back fat, with or without some meat in it, similar to pancetta, but heavily smoked and salted, and sometimes sprinkled with paprika. We ate it with bread and onions, but only in small amounts because it was quite heavy on the stomach. In summer, when we had barbecues out in the fields, we used to put pieces of *slanina* on a skewer and drip fat onto large slices of home-made bread. It has a very distinctive taste which I always associate now with childhood family time and summer fun. My Mum fries small pieces to add to omelettes, soups, or as additional flavour to polenta dishes.

Villagers are practical and industrious people, but they also appreciate the beauty of 'Mother Nature' all around them. When I was young there was a smaller garden in front of the house for decorative flowers. We used to make bouquets to take to church on Sundays, or to decorate the family room for religious celebrations. Daffodils, hyacinths and tulips appeared in spring, followed by roses, carnations and bell flowers in summer, then dahlias and chrysanthemums emerged in autumn. These days I prefer single colour bouquets, but at that time we were mixing whatever was available, in what would today be called a rather bohemian floral arrangement.

Today's buzzwords like 'organic', 'bio', 'biodynamic', 'free range', 'regenerative farming' for which city dwellers are willing to pay premium prices, are the norm in Transylvania. For centuries before I was born, and still to a fairly large extent today, everything was homegrown, organically fertilised and eaten in season. It is a far cry from life in the big cities of the world, where people rarely know the origins of their food, and processed or chemically treated food is often the only affordable choice.

Certainly, no one went hungry in Manastireni. Recipes were simple but hearty and never pretentious, just like the people. There are to this day four stalwart condiments - salt, pepper, sweet paprika and fresh parsley. Sometimes dill would get a look in.

With most food cooked on the day the farm kitchen is a constant hubbub of activity. There's always a pot cooking. At Christmas and Easter women go into overdrive, preparing a dizzying array of dishes for large gatherings of family and friends. Hosting is a big part of the local culture, so expect the table to be overflowing with starters, mains that are impossible to finish and then, the coup de grace, mouth - watering homemade cakes arrive when everyone is too full to speak or move. They are all delicious and you will be eagerly watched as you try everything!

A plentiful table indicates a host's prosperity, as do big hips for women and a big belly for men, or so it was in Grandma's youth. She was a tall, slim lady all her life, and she confessed to adding additional layers of underskirts to make her hips look wider.

If we ever had fish it was trout from streams half an hour higher up the mountain, but it wasn't very often, and the local shop didn't stock it regularly. The village stream and river were not deep enough to have big fish to eat, but they were great for fun fishing with my friends. We would catch tiny fish and feed them to the cat or simply release them.

A snack in our village would be pork fat spread on a hearty piece of home-made bread; the slice normally larger than my face. I discovered something similar in Bavaria later on when I attended a friend's wedding and it made me smile, thinking of my long - lost childhood delight. Today I would never imagine eating that, but at that time we craved it.

Soups are incredibly diverse, influenced by the various cultures that have crossed this land throughout history. The soup menu in a traditional restaurant is often just as long as the meat dishes. There are the clear soups – chicken noodle, meat dumplings *perisoare*, and semolina and egg dumplings *galuste*. *Ciorba* is a thicker broth-type soup made sweet with potatoes, tomatoes and meat; some people add sour cream to it. In summer popular options are either lettuce, cabbage or nettle soup, cooked with pieces of fried *slanina* and sour cream. Delicious!

Everywhere you go in Transylvania, and indeed the whole of Romania, you will come across tripe soup known as *ciorba de burta*. It is a very difficult recipe to get right, but when done well is a yellow, creamy, sour mix with slices of cow stomach, served with bread and a hot green pepper, to help cut through the fat and richness of the broth. My family never ventured to cook this at home. I have only enjoyed it in restaurants.

Main dishes are all about potatoes in different forms, and meat is largely a mix of pork and chicken, with lamb served at Easter. Do not leave Transylvania without trying a stew or *tocana*. It is extremely tasty, like a goulash or a mild curry, with fried onions, meat and vegetables in tomato sauce, using the classic quartet of condiments. If making it yourself, you have to be patient and cook it at low to moderate heat for more than an hour so the flavours can merge together.

Another local delicacy is *sarmale*, vine or cabbage leaves stuffed with a mix of rice and meat, similar to the Greek dolmades. People eat them with bread and sour cream. They are another one of those all-day cooking affairs that the local cuisine often requires. If anything, the Transylvanian kitchen teaches one patience!

Something to get used to for many people is that everything is consumed with bread, even potato and rice dishes. Romanians take bread to whole new levels. The country has one of the highest levels of bread consumption per capita in Europe, of more than eighty kilograms a year, and that is just the bread sold in shops! A lot of people, especially in villages, still bake their own, a quantity unaccounted for in official statistics. The highest protocol of welcoming a guest in Romania is to be greeted by an official alongside someone in traditional costume carrying bread and salt.

Bread loaves come in many shapes – from the traditional bloomer baked in a moulded tin, to a boule, a baton, a local croissant shape known as *corn*, roll, cob, or a challah-type bread known as *colac*. The *colac* is generally cooked for big events and celebrations – whether public, religious or family-related ones. You will often see them in Transylvanian churches with candles stuck in them when the priest is conducting a blessing.

Newlyweds receive a piece of bread dipped in honey to wish them a sweet life. No house ever runs out of bread. When Grandma baked her own, the loaf was so big and dense that it would last more than a week and not go stale. The baking is done in artisanal clay or brick ovens. The crust is so thick you have to cut it off, and the aroma is simply delicious.

If you have a sweet tooth like me, you will love *cozonac*, loosely the dessert version of *colac*. For this recipe you add milk, eggs, sugar and a filling of walnuts. It is a classic delicacy for Christmas and Easter, but it isn't taken to church and no candles are involved. Since Grandma didn't have a kneading machine to make the dough, home baking *cozonac* was a serious affair and did not happen often. It meant her starting her day around 4am to prepare the dough. It took a lot of effort to knead it by hand. She would finish by the time we woke up and would let the yeast work its magic until midday before popping it in the oven. As a child I was not allowed to touch the dough at any stage other than when it was about to go in the oven, Grandma didn't want anything to interfere with the yeast.

Even my Mum, who is an excellent cook and baker, has never attempted making *cozonac* and she is in her sixties. I do encourage you to taste it. Each region has slight variations in the filling recipe, so you might taste cocoa, jam or Turkish delight in the walnut paste. You can eat it plain or the way I like it - warmed up alongside a glass of milk or a cup of coffee. I hope you will savour it as much as I do.

Where is the cheese you might ask? Well, everywhere and very fresh! There is little processing involved, especially in the countryside recipes. Milk from cows, sheep, goats and sometimes buffalo is drunk immediately or turned into cheese. *Urda* and *cas* are fresh cheeses, similar to ricotta; *branza de vaca* is like cottage cheese but comes shaped like a hard ball. Then there is *telemea* which is a feta equivalent. *Branza de burduf* is *cas* mixed with salt and left to age in fir tree bark, so it may taste slightly spicy. *Cascaval* is the commercial version, like a mild cheddar or mozzarella. You will often see the latter on restaurant menus served breaded and fried. A farmers' market is the best place to find all these variations. Cold starter platters are usually a mix of cheeses, *slanina* and sausages or cold meats. This can also be served as breakfast.

Vegetarians are not forgotten in Transylvania. It is a meat heavy region, make no mistake, but you can also find delicious dishes that are meat free. The classic *sarmale* come meat free if you ask for *sarmale de post*, cabbage rolls stuffed with rice. *Ciorba taraneasca* is a vegetable soup that is widely available. Most Fridays growing up we would have bean soup *ciorba de fasole* or bean paste *fasole frecata* for lunch and the farmers' staple polenta *mamaliga* for dinner. You will in fact find *mamaliga* eaten hot or cold, with and without *slanina* or cheese. *Zacusca* is a mix of vegetables made of sauteed onions, tomatoes and peppers and sometimes grilled aubergines. Along with an aubergine dip called *salata de vinete* they are well-known cold starters; sometimes they are served for breakfast on homemade bread. Special occasions called for another starter recipe of peppers stuffed with rice and cooked in the oven, *ardei umpluti*. When in season people also rush to cook mushroom dishes that are extremely tasty and carry a strong aroma.

A particular summer favourite with incredible flavour is the local watermelon. You will see producers selling them on the side of the road, guarding hundreds of them in one place. My father would always be careful to buy from the people who had the biggest piles, meaning they had just arrived at their spot and the watermelon had not been sitting there for too long.

Whatever your eating habits may be, one thing to note is that you will be expected to eat a lot more than usual and nobody will take no for an answer.

Pofta buna - enjoy your meal and remember to pace yourself!

Man's Best Friends

Subsistence farming is still the norm in Transylvania and animals play a huge part in everyone's lives. From horses to sheep, from cows to poultry, every family has a few animals to look after, and they do so like they are their own children.

When Radu and Jicu, the two horses on my Grandpa's farm, turned one year old, they were sent up into the Apuseni Mountains to Belis Lake. They spent four months there, toughening up in the mountain air, before starting work on the farm. The villagers paid someone a fee to look after the animals so they wouldn't go too far, given that there are no fences and the horses were free to graze where they pleased around the lake. When it was time to bring them back, Grandpa and my uncle walked ten miles to the lake and then rode them home, ready to use them on the farm. This sojourn served them well and made them two of the strongest horses in the village.

They were both Lipizaners: strong, robust horses weighing half a ton each. Historically, the breed was brought to the region by the Hapsburgs, descendants of Spanish horses, and were used by the army, postal service and noblemen. They mixed with local breeds as well and created a very intelligent, hard- working, and quick-learning horse. Exactly what was needed for the Transylvanian terrain and farming activities.

Radu and Jicu were very good at sensing wolves, which would sometimes approach the village looking for food, especially in winter. A sure sign of a wolf nearby would be the horses facing each other, head to head, ready to kick with their rear legs. These wolves have never come close enough for us to be in danger, but I could see them at the back of the house on a distant hilltop and was aware how the horses would signal their presence. As children we were regularly reminded to be vigilant.

Because he was gentler than Jicu, I proclaimed Radu my horse and took extra care of him. He was the lucky recipient of thicker blankets, a larger supply of Jonathan apples as a treat, a bigger pile of hay and fresh water; I really went the extra mile for him. Jicu scared easily so we all had to remember never to approach him from behind. He had to see you otherwise you would get kicked, like our neighbour Daniel did one spring. Over the summer, they would spend the night out in the open air on the village pasture, with just a piece of rope tied to their front hooves. Neither of them would leave the village without Grandpa, so we never really had to worry about them running away. The village pasture didn't have enclosures either; all animals were free to roam as they wished.

Every season brought different tasks. Summer was for hay work, and spring and autumn was for spreading manure and ploughing. Autumn was also the time of the harvest. We always seemed to be moving something from one place to another as the seasons changed. In winter the horses transported the stacks of hay from the fields back to the barn or lugged additional logs for winter fires.

At the time very few families owned tractors, maybe only one or two in every village, so everyone used horse-drawn carts. Now that smaller tractors are available and also more affordable, more people buy them. Only the older generation, or those without means, still use their carts.

Transporting logs by cart was a serious effort for the animals, and all the more reason to look after them very carefully. In Communist times, before the revolution which deposed President Ceausescu in 1989, the Cooperative would allocate a certain number of trees in the forest to each family who lived in the mountains. Grandpa would have his trees cut down in spring and turned into lumber planks, then he would transport and sell them in the villages on the plains, travelling as far as 100 km from home. This meant being away for two weeks at a time with his horses and his cart. He slept in the cart and lived on a diet of *slanina* and smoked sausages, tinned meat and bread. The men from the village would travel in groups of five to ten carts.

There was always a risk of being attacked at night, as the thieves knew that no lumber in the cart meant money in their pockets. Luckily nothing serious happened to Grandpa all the years he did this. The horses knew the routes so well that even when he was asleep the animals would just keep walking. They had learned the way home and didn't need direction. Grandma and I recognised the sound of their hooves in the night and would open the gates so they could come straight into the yard without having to wait for a single moment. Afterwards, Grandpa would tell us stories from his trip every evening for weeks. I often asked him to recount some of my favourite stories from his previous trips too. It was our version of bedtime reading with real life adventure tales.

My grandparents had to milk the cows twice a day, at the crack of dawn and in the evening. I tried to help a few times, but no milk would come out, I clearly didn't grasp the technique, neither did I try too hard. I was happy to let them do it for me. The milk was so rich we had to scoop the cream off the top in order to get a drink. The cats also made a beeline for the barn when it was time for fresh milk.

From around the end of April to October, the cows would leave the farm at five in the morning and join the others, belonging to other families, to graze on the village pasture all day. Sometimes goats would join them, but not many families had goats in that area. Afterwards the farmers could get on with their daily chores around the home or out in the fields. The animals would come back at sundown, ready to be milked, and then everything would happen all over again the next day. Even today you will see villagers leaving the gates open in the evening for the animals to wander home, the 'Cows' Parade'. It was a lovely, free life for the animals when they were not at work.

In Durusa, there aren't as many animals left today, the young have left the village to live in nearby cities. The land where my Dad used to take the family cows to pasture hosts an increasingly popular international music festival called Durusa Summer Hills. I'm glad my cousins thought of this event to open the area to the wider world and I hope it will stay successful and expand in the future.

Because the local diet includes a lot of pork, most families raise their own pigs. They are fattened up from spring until December, then slaughtered in time for Christmas and New Year feasts. No part of the pig goes to waste: from the

meat to the blood, from the ears to the fat. Sausages are smoked to last for months and some meat is frozen. *Slanina* is hung in the attic, to be used later for ploughman's lunches in the fields. Every household prides itself on how they raise their pigs. Grandma never revealed the recipe for her pig feed, but it was a mix of bran, nettles, boiled water, fresh milk and grains. Only she knew the proportions. As my grandparents never went on holiday, she didn't have to reveal her recipe to anyone. My parents didn't keep pigs or any other animals after she passed away so that mix is gone forever.

Sheep farming is an ancient tradition in Transylvania, dating back to Roman times. Transhumance, which means moving the sheep across large distances to graze is still alive, albeit losing its appeal and practicality in the modern world. Transylvania is one of the few parts of Europe where it still happens. Sheep are valued for their meat and milk. Their wool is relatively coarse so it is not widely used for commercial purposes. Romania has the third highest count of sheep in the EU, estimated at around eleven million. You will invariably come across them as you travel around. Although no set transhumance routes exist, shepherds know their way around and how to avoid busy areas.

Farmers are happy for the sheep to cross their lands as they provide a natural fertiliser for their crops. They can't pull out the roots as they graze the stubble since they have no top incisor teeth. This is an example of the symbiotic agro-ecological lifestyle practiced in Transylvania. The only thing between the sheep and the forest beasts is the coral the shepherds create, to keep all the sheep close at night. The shepherd dogs guard the sheep and the men have sticks, but not guns. They respect nature and the dangers and are willing to accept the risks that come with the environment.

Historically, shepherds would cover up to three hundred kilometers per flock in a year, but nowadays short distance transhumance is practiced, either within the region or just around the villages. Nowadays shepherds are away for weeks at a time only if they are in high-altitude areas, as it is too time consuming to keep coming down to the valley floor daily.

There is a strict daily routine with the sheep being milked three times a day. Cheese is made on the spot, then put in barrels and other wooden containers

carried by donkeys. The end product is as natural and organic as it comes, with no pasteurisation or other chemicals. With EU regulations focused on hygiene and packaging, this practice of making cheese is under threat. Locals don't pay too much attention to this for now; this cheese doesn't reach commercial stores, it's simply consumed fresh as soon as it's produced, as people have done for centuries. They know the natural microbes from this cheese are a stimulus for their immune systems.

In Manastireni, most families had up to ten sheep, and there was a rota for the farmers to take their share of milk and cheese home every few days. Sometimes that meant a fun donkey ride to collect it, but sadly I didn't get to join Grandpa as the collection run was done late in the evening, after all the day's work was done and the cows were milked. He would be gone for half the night.

The share of milk and cheese for each family would be calculated each spring, after all the animals were first taken to pasture for a week or two. On a set day, the villagers would join the shepherds to witness their respective sheep being milked. The shepherds would mark down the milk production of each family's sheep, then the allocation was calculated, and it remained that way for the rest of the season. The practice is followed to this day although the sheep headcount is lower every year.

When it comes to dogs, the farmers don't care so much about the pedigree. They just want them to be strong and loyal. The local breed of Carpathian or Romanian shepherd dogs are just that. Their origin goes back to Dacian times, almost two thousand years ago. They are intelligent, hard-working, protective animals, very loving to their owners, suspicious of strangers, and ready to fight wild animals. They are one of the only dog breeds known to be able to fight bears, not alone, but in packs. They live outdoors, revelling in lots of exercise, and are perfect for life on the farm.

My paternal grandparents owned several such dogs over the years and we got very attached to them. Azor, their dog in the 1980s would religiously accompany Grandpa everywhere. One day, as he went to mow some grass in a nearby garden, the dog laid down to sleep by a basket with Grandpa's things in it. At lunchtime Grandpa came home, got busy with other things and didn't return to the field. That evening they realised the dog was missing but didn't think anything of it. He often wandered off and returned at some point in the evening or night. The next day, while working elsewhere a villager told him: 'Hey, Vasile, why did you leave your dog in Ograda Tomii? I could barely cross your land to get to mine. That dog is so vicious!'. Sure enough, when Grandpa made his way back to the garden of the day prior, Azor was in the same spot, loyally guarding all of his things, a full day later.

Tambur joined our family in the 1990s once Grandpa had passed away. He was a very large dog, raised on a diet of fresh cow's milk twice a day and homemade bread. Tambur was very loyal to Grandma and followed her everywhere. When she went to the post office to collect her pension every month, he would be the first to walk into the building, as if to check for danger. Being such a large dog, everyone would move away, clearing the path for Grandma who then would have no wait. The ladies at the front desk recognised the dog and prepared Grandma's money right away.

Tambur was also very protective of all the animals on the farm, once they were introduced to him. With every generation of new chicks or piglets, we would bring each of them to Tambur's nose, let him gently sniff them, and after that he would stop chasing them. When it was time for one of the cows to be sold, Grandma locked him in the barn and she went to market in the nearby town of Somcuta Mare. They were worried he wouldn't allow the cow to leave the village. While chatting to potential buyers at the market Grandma noticed Tambur appear out of nowhere and lay down without making a sound in front of the cow. They later discovered the dog had broken through the locked barn gate and walked ten miles to find them. Once the cow was sold, my Dad had to place a loaf of bread in the car to encourage Tambur to get in as he had never been in a car before. He held the bread in his mouth for the entire journey back and only ate it once he was back at the farm. Over the years he learned Grandma's comings and goings and would always run ahead, then back to Grandma, as if to signal safe passage.

The careful balance between man, animals and nature will go on for as long as small farms are still running. This symbiosis with nature is not an expression, it's a way of life in Transylvania.

Craftsmanship

ALL THE TRADITIONS of Transylvania date back centuries. These ancient practices can be seen in the handicrafts of the region. From woodwork to embroidery to pottery, and even Easter egg decorations, things which one might expect to find in a museum are still made by local artisans and used in people's daily lives.

We are at an inflection point in history when many of these century old crafts face extinction as artisans disappear and their skills are not passed on. We need to find ways to inspire, educate and encourage new generations of individuals to perpetuate these valuable skills and elements of the local identity.

The Heritage Crafts Association is the UK advocacy body for traditional crafts. In 2017 they published a ranking of crafts by their probability to survive this generation, the first time such an undertaking had taken place. The Association also lobbies the government to see crafts as part of a nation's cultural heritage and to put measures in place to pass these skills to the new generations.

There has never been a shortage of wood in the region. Local craftsmen have had centuries to perfect their skills. Everything from farm fences and gates, from utensils to furniture is made of solid wood. Maramures is a region known particularly for its imposing sculpted wooden gates. Each large gate comprises three pillars and is made wide enough for carts to go through. Up until the 1930s, only noble men were allowed to erect such a gate to denote their status. I'm not sure at what point this rule was dropped and why, but the desire for ornate gates has continued, and people today take great pride in the style and design showcased by their property. Depending on the level of detail in the sculpted elements, one order can take several months to carve, and it can cost more than thirty thousand euros.

Gates can depict religious symbols, or scenes from village life: for example people working the land, or single elements such as wheat sheaves, the sun, fish, fir trees, ram horns, or geometrical shapes like diamonds and spirals. Each has its own significance and the origins go back to pre-Christian times. The sun is a symbol of life and the rope depicts the connection between sky and earth. The same intricate carvings can also be found on dowry chests, doors, and even garden implements and musical instruments.

Inside the farmhouses of Transylvania all the furniture is made of wood, carved in a wide range of designs, incorporating spirals, waves, rosettes and crosses. Sometimes this wood is painted and adorned with flowers, an influence from the Saxon settlers in the southeastern corner of Transylvania going back to the Middle Ages. Saxons were strong fighters and protected Transylvania from continuous invasions. The Saxon culture soon merged with the Transylvanian culture, and although there are far fewer Saxon descendants today, most of them moved to Germany after the fall of communism, their influence remains.

You might encounter wooden sculpted crosses at crossroads as you drive around. They are called *troite* and are meant to protect travellers and shepherds from evil spirits.

Textile work, and embroidery in particular, is extremely intricate, with motif designs passed down from one generation to the next. Each region has its own characteristics. A century ago, everything inside the traditional farmhouse was handmade, including carpets, towels and blankets. The materials were mainly wool and bast fibres like hemp and flax. Bast fibres come from the various surrounding plants or trees and are used to make matting and cord. Hemp is non-allergenic, highly resistant to rotting and to UV light. It doesn't go yellow and doesn't stretch at all. While we admire their talent, the rural population perfected their craft out of necessity. There were no shops, or not enough money to buy such things. They simply had to work with what was available locally.

Such traditions have taken a lot longer to peter out compared to other parts of Europe, due to the fact that the rural communities have focused on preserving their elders' traditions and as a direct consequence of having limited means or ties to the wider outside world. The village was their entire universe.

In the Transylvania of my grandparents' youth, just as men were not deemed ready to marry until they knew how to build a house, women had to know how to cook, and how to weave all the items for the house. Weaving was done in winter when the field work was less demanding. Nowadays, you can still see elderly Transylvanian residents wearing traditional handmade clothing. Work clothes are quite plain, but the Sunday outfits are heavily decorated or embroidered, with starched blouses for ceremonies and church. Sunday clothes are kept separate and carefully looked after.

The traditional Romanian blouse, the *ie* or *ia*, has been embraced by the younger generations who pair it with more modern items of clothing. The colours and motifs are quite diverse depending on the region, and the embroidery detail is exquisite. As you travel across the various counties that make up Transylvania you will notice the designs change.

The folk costumes of this region have served as inspiration for countless fashion designers and artists, from Yves Saint Laurent to Lacroix, Dior to Tory Burch, Valentino to Tom Ford to name just a few. The Romanian blouse has developed a social media following and digital community of its own, called *La Blouse Roumaine* and the founder Andreea Tanasescu has embarked on an important global mission to inspire designers to give credit to the cultural communities they draw inspiration from.

Head scarves worn by married women can be very colourful, black is reserved for widows and the elderly. Aprons are another piece of the rural costume with a wide variety of designs and colours.

Men's shirts tend to be fairly similar from one region to another, white and generally made of hemp or flax, wider at the bottom than at the shoulders, and quite long, almost down to the knee. Men's trousers have more variation, from quite skinny-legged in the Apuseni Mountains area to very wide, baggy style in Maramures. In winter, a sheepskin coat called a *cojoc* keeps both men and women warm. They are extremely heavy. As a child I could barely lift one up to help my Grandma get dressed. These are generally left in the natural colours of the wool, either white, grey or beige.

Hats are made of lamb's wool and are worn all year except for summer. Men are even buried wearing them.

My favourite male garment is the reverse sheepskin vest called a *pieptar*. It has to be scoured, softened and then oiled to be waterproof, before being extensively embroidered. They are all personalised to the owner. Some people even add fur trim for an added special touch. They are quite something when finished, and I feel lucky to own a few in my personal collection.

Felted wool is used for coats, slippers, boots and hats. It is especially useful as it can be sewn edge to edge, with no need for a hem as it doesn't fray. The added advantage is that felting makes wool thicker and water repellent. Once the wool is woven or knitted, the fabric is splashed with hot water, forcing the fibres to lock together, then beaten for hours to make it thick and compact. To complete their costume men also use a broad belt with small pockets and holes called a *chimir*.

It can take months to make some of these items, and with the passage of time the number of skilled artisans capable of creating them is drastically diminishing. In some places this knowledge is already lost. Most villagers are now buying factory made clothes and keep the traditional dress for church and for important family celebrations. A noteworthy project comes from fashion brand MA RA MI. Designer Andra Clitan worked with traditional craftsmen from Maramures to create a collection using natural fabrics such as wool, with traditional motifs from different parts of Romania. This work became an art installation called 'A Wool Journey' that showcased the entire process of processing wool. It is a great example of how designers today can shine a light on the crafts of an area and bring historical methods into contemporary life and fashion.

Decorating Easter eggs is another tradition going back centuries. The local women employ a variety of motifs and colours using vegetables and other natural dyes. The decorations are done by drawing with melted beeswax and dipping into multiple dye baths until the desired colour combination is reached. On Easter morning the tradition says you should pair with another member of the family or guest and hit the eggs against each other saying: 'Christ has risen'. The response is: 'He has risen indeed.' The person whose egg hasn't cracked is believed to live the longest.

If you happen to have an egg with two yolks, then it's believed you will get married soon or there will be a wedding in the family.

Some other specialised village crafts from the past are ironmongery, skinning and ceramic artistry. Manastireni had only one iron monger, and his craft stayed in his family for several generations until the last member passed away in the 1990s. All our horses had their shoes made there.

Skinners were scattered throughout the region in larger villages and towns. The gilets and coats made this way were one of the only items of clothing not produced in the farmers' homes. These artisans are also mostly gone, testament being the difficulty in finding a *cojoc* today.

Ceramic and pottery casting is a tradition with over two thousand years of history. There are villages and towns all over Transylvania where you can find artisans at work. It is probably the most preserved skill from the past. The most famous village for ceramics and pottery is Corund in the south but worth mentioning are also the ceramic centres of Baia Mare, Cluj, Sibiu, Brasov, Bistrita, and Dej. The products range from plates, jugs and bowls to use in the house, to decorative objects for terracotta stoves. The main colors used are brown, green, yellow and ochre, and in some areas blue. Corund is particularly known for its specific colours and shapes - tulips, edelweiss or the male wood grouse. In this village alone there are more than one hundred potters. They also produce a well-known black ceramic.

Notable craftsmen are also those working with corn husks, wicker and hazel twigs to create anything from furniture and baskets, to bottle covers and bread holders. It is another dying art, however at traditional fairs or in village museums you can still find stalls selling these products.

The mentality of the people of Transylvania serves the crafts industry well. A local saying says: 'Don't start anything if you're not going to do it properly.' I encourage you to find something to take home and help perpetuate these skills for future generations of craftsmen and women. They are the distillation of centuries of skill building, and reflect a nation's traditions and influences.

These crafts were once omnipresent and now are the object of the few, those who persevered, and who cannot imagine doing anything else. We cannot lose this part of the national identity. How can we inspire this slow craft movement for the future? What are some realistic and practical ways to keep these traditions alive? Could we have creative retreats for designers and artists to mix with local artisans, drop in *sezatoare* in village halls on select dates, workshops for children, or even online courses. This way we wouldn't displace communities and design and craft communities could collaborate and reinterpret traditional items to become objects of desire for the new bohemians, people in search for products that tell a story, and depict a sense of place.

Blue

IN A GAME of matching colours to places, in my mind, Transylvania would get blue. I always think of this colour when I think of home. The sky, rivers, lakes, but also the vernacular houses, the local embroidery, furniture, religious icons, pottery. The list of objects and places where blue is prevalent can be very long.

There are various theories why blue is so popular. It isn't really a forest colour after all. Some sources claim it keeps evil away, blue being the colour of divinity. Greeks believe this too, and since Transylvania shares the same Orthodox religion as Greece this could constitute a valid reason. Blue is also one of the three colours of the Romanian flag. Another theory is that in the Middle Ages, when Transylvania was under Austro-Hungarian rule, the local Romanian farmers would paint their houses blue, to differentiate themselves from Hungarians, who painted their houses green. However, green houses are not numerous enough to fully embrace this theory.

I am inclined to believe the religious explanation, since it goes back many more centuries, and reflects the strong deference to God and church in Transylvania, especially in the countryside. In the 12th century, images used in churches included blue elements. Virgin Mary's clothes are blue; the ceiling, if painted, has vast areas of blue; the walls, even in wooden churches, are often painted with this colour. Blue is associated with heaven and freedom. Furthermore, Central European folk culture considers blue to signify loyalty, but also mysterious and uncertain things.

Icons found in churches, replicas of which are often adopted inside farmers' homes as decoration, also favour this colour. Blue is often used by the artists painting on glass, a tradition going back two to three hundred years. It's a technique learned from the West, during the Habsburg rule and employed

by local artists to paint religious scenes. These works can be found in areas around Brasov, Sibiu, Fagaras and Nicula (Cluj county); thus, a fair distribution all over Transylvania.

In the village of Sapanta in northern Maramures, a few miles from the border with Ukraine, you can discover the 'Sapanta Blue'. It is a collection of crosses in the UNESCO - protected Merry Cemetery. The life of each person buried there is depicted in a humorous way on wooden carvings, painted on a deep blue background and using other vivid colours. It is a very humbling experience to stand in the middle of the cemetery and marvel at the talent and vision which created them.

To paint the farmhouses blue, original whitewash formula was mixed with copper sulphate. The process required some forward planning in order to get to this end result. Farmers would dig a hole in the ground in autumn, fill it with quicklime and water (one kilo or two pounds of quicklime to nine litres of water) then wait until spring when the lime putty is mature enough to be used for limewash paint. It works as an antiseptic agent as well and its popularity goes back to Roman times or maybe even prior. Should you mix lime putty with clay, you have a breathable, flexible insulation agent. Another self-sufficiency example in action since quicklime and clay are available materials all over the region at little cost.

For centuries, Transylvania has been a melting pot of nationalities and cultures. Every ethnic group which has sought refuge or fortune in Transylvania has left its mark on the local culture. The traditional blue pottery comes from the Habans, a group of Protestant craftsmen, exiled from Hungary, but with their roots in Switzerland and Austria. They settled in central Transylvania in the 17th century, later moving further east. Their floral pattern pottery was influenced by the ceramic of Delft. They used a high-quality paint recipe and exchanged ideas and techniques with local potters. It was a time when ceramic objects were being cherished for their style as well as their function, enriching Transylvanian interior design. Water pitchers, jugs and plates started appearing in the towns of Cluj and Gherla, the white backgrounds adorned by floral and vegetal motifs. The practice of mixing east and west techniques and designs were to live to the present day.

The people of Transylvania used natural dyes until the end of the 19th century and early into the 20th century, when these were replaced by chemical alternatives. Women used various leaves, flowers, roots, tree bark and some minerals like alumen kalikum and calcium hydroxide. Like so many things, the dye mixes were passed down from generation to generation, rarely written down. Local folklore researchers have recorded more than three hundred paint recipes – ninety each for black and yellow, sixty - two for red, forty - four for green, twenty - nine for blue and eighteen recipes for white. Transylvanians still use natural dyes for Easter egg colours - red onion peel for red, red cabbage for blue, beetroot juice for pink, spinach leaves for, you guessed it, green.

Transylvania is a riot of colour wherever one looks, with blue taking centre stage, and there is a sense of serenity in knowing it has always been that way.

Village Life

THE ROMANIAN POET Lucian Blaga said: 'Eternity was born in the village'. There are some places in this world which breathe and live with you; places where moral and spiritual values are paramount. A world where the land is a part of you. That is rural Transylvania.

The pace of life is slower than in the surrounding towns and cities, and people who live in these small communities may even speak more slowly. They are renowned regionally for being calm, and not speaking if they have nothing specific to say.

I noticed the differences in the pace of speaking when I left Transylvania to study at the opposite end of the country, in the capital of Romania, Bucharest. People could definitely put me on the map, and they seemed impatient for me to finish my sentences. Transylvanians have a saying for those who talk a lot - *Sezi bland* – which would be loosely translated by the British as 'Keep Calm'.

That doesn't mean they don't communicate well. Villagers enjoy keeping up with each other's news and chatting about the things which matter most to them, especially at the market, after church, or sitting on benches in front of their homes in the evening. There are shortcuts in every village which cross people's courtyards and gardens, and villagers will stop for a chat with whomever they meet on the way. Everyone knows everyone. The priest, the postman, the doctor and local police officers are always 'in the know' and a great source of updates.

There are no newspapers being delivered to villages. Most elders haven't gone past primary school with their studies, so people take their news by talking to each other and from TV or radio. During my childhood, any news of importance to the entire village would be communicated by a man walking up and down with a drum and shouting his announcement. As children we found this extremely exciting, his voice was booming!

At my Mum's family home, the Saturday market was just down the road from our house, as Manastireni is one of the largest villages around. On my Dad's side, Durusa was a much smaller settlement, slightly isolated, on top of a hill, at the edge of a forest, and ten miles from the nearest market town. This didn't stop my Grandma to be an avid seller all her life, and she would go to the market in Somcuta Mare every Monday to sell her cheese, sour cream, plum brandy and walnuts. She would then buy or barter for whatever else she needed on the farm. She knew the price of everything, from cows to sugar, and tractors.

The bigger villages organised dances on Sundays to coincide with religious celebrations. They would start after church mass was over. Music is a well-loved tradition in the countryside, particularly folk music, yet another reason for the community to come together. The elders sit on the sidelines and watch every step and smile the youngsters make. They discuss marriage options to the ignorance of the younger generation. Ask your host if there are any events in the area that you could attend. A party is always a party, regardless of the community size or continent, and I guarantee you will have a memorable experience.

During summer, families with a lot of land organise *claca*, a day, or several days, where men from the village join in to help one particular farmer with his chores. Working together means finishing faster, and they then move on to the next farm in need. Sometimes groups of men travel throughout the region and offer their services for a day or two to finish major tasks like mowing by hand. They sleep in the barn and can work from dawn until sunset, with their meals prepared by the women of the household. Every hour of daylight is used and there is only a quick stop for lunch.

During winter, when the intense field work stops, women used to organise *sezatoare*, an evening gathering meant for socialising, but also for showing off their beautiful, comfortable homes and traditional talents. Girls showcase their skills in front of potential suitors. Families take turns in hosting their neighbours. Women weave, knit, sing, tell stories and riddles and for larger gatherings there's even dancing. If you're lucky to have some of the village's oldest women join in, then they can use magic pre-Christian rituals to predict the future. For example, they might set light to leftover hemp and throw the pieces on the floor. The first girl that the hemp pieces move towards will get married that year.

Nowadays the tradition of *sezatoare* is followed sporadically, depending on the size of the community and level of commitment for traditional activities.

Marriage is an extremely important ritual in the villages given it can determine the fate of the family land. Everyone pays close attention to how much land each person has; their work ethic; their reputation; their personality and even their drinking habits. Marriages are not arranged like in some other parts of the world, where the pair might not even know each other. But merging land ownership is still a goal. Both sets of my grandparents ended up being together because their families decided it was best to put their lands together and the work ethic on all sides was considered the right one. Neither couple had established strong bonds before their respective weddings, but they came from similar backgrounds in the same village, and later worked hard together to look after their land and send their children to university. They were good matches and stayed together until their last days.

I am under no illusion that life in the countryside was and is tough, but it didn't seem that way growing up. Everybody worked hard and had enough supplies, or they bartered to make ends meet. Work in the field followed set patterns and rules depending on the season; people knew how things worked and followed what previous generations had done and when.

The dynamic has changed in the last twenty years, as new generations have moved away, and the elders are no longer physically able to carry out the hard labour required every season. Some EU funds are being channelled through to some degree but not in a consistent manner across the territory. There is a formal process to submit funding requests that villagers won't master unless they employ the services of a professional. It will be interesting to follow whether a balance can be struck between the pull of the cities and the opportunities in the countryside.

I would love to inspire socially conscious tourists or the curious minds around us to get involved with these communities or plan their travels in this part of the world. I am a fan of the Transylvanian Brunch, a regular weekend gathering that is organised in various villages throughout the year and a way to discover new places, meet the locals, try forgotten recipes and enjoy the outdoors. More and more popular are cycling tours throughout southern Transylvania and around the Saxon villages, a wonderful example of slow tourism that blends exercise, local food, beautiful scenery and traditions. The new wave of travellers seek more and more unique experiences and they will find them abundantly in Transylvania!

Superstitions and Traditions

THE COMPLICATED HISTORY of Transylvania, with its many rulers and invaders, has kept communities close - knit over the centuries. Sharing the Orthodox religion and attending the same church every Sunday has fostered a strong joint belief system. Some of these beliefs are in reality superstitions, encompassing theories about the world around us - from birds to animals, from people to money and love. Certain dates of the year give rise to particular superstitions. You will find that the smaller the community, the stronger these beliefs.

Here are a few examples of the things I was told as a child and, of course, believed completely.

If you're still in bed when the sun is up, you'll have a bad day.

If you take down a stork's nest, it will set fire to your house.

If hares come close to the village, you'll have a long winter.

Don't give out money on a Monday or you'll lose money all week. However, it's good to receive money on a Monday, as it means you'll get money all week.

If your left palm itches, you'll receive money. If it's your right palm, you will give money.

Don't spill black pepper, otherwise you'll have a fight with somebody.

Don't stand in the doorway, or it will rain on your wedding day.

Many mice around the farm means a rich harvest, or a rich year ahead, or a long winter.

What you dream about on the day of St Thomas ('Ziua Tomii', the first Sunday after Easter Sunday) will come true.

If you work on the St Peter's day ('Sf. Petru', 29 June) you will lose money.

In my Dad's village of Durusa, farmers used to lay a chain by the stable door for a newborn calf to step over the first time it went outside. It was meant to ensure that the animal would grow as strong as the chain.

The positioning of the farmhouse is very important. No one would want to build a house on land believed to carry a spell, or close to a crime scene. Abandoned houses are considered bad places, haunted by spirits. Doorways and gutters are places of transition, from the real world into the world of the dead, so ornaments or plants are placed around them to keep evil spirits away.

Crossroads outside villages carry bad omens as spirits travel across these roads. Religious crosses and fountains are placed in these locations, to bring good luck. No village elder will build a house near crossroads if given the choice. If people believe a certain place has a bad omen, they will purposely avoid it, and also keep their animals away from it.

When starting a new job, Mondays and Thursdays are considered good days, Tuesdays and Fridays less so. There's no sowing on religious celebration days. In some villages, when a plough is taken out for the first time in spring, the farmer attaches a bread loaf to the plough as a symbol of prosperity to come.

Cows and sheep come with a long list of superstitions and actions necessary to protect them from evil spirits, wolves or even bad weather. For example, placing garlic or lovage leaves by stable doors can help.

And there are so many more. When I was young, both sets of my grandparents were often quoting proverbs to keep kids in line and to instil discipline.

Here are a few of the ones I remember.

Hit while the iron is hot.

Talk too much, you'll end up poor. (which obviously meant that if we were talking, then we were not working!)

He who chases two rabbits gets none.

Don't look a gift horse in the mouth.

A cat with a bell never catches mice.

After the war, lots of brave men appear.

As you can see, many proverbs promote working hard, minding your own business, talking less and doing more.

Silence is golden.

Don't leave for tomorrow what you can do today.

If you don't work during the day, you will be hungry at night.

Leave early in the morning to go far.

Keep what you have in your hand as it's not a lie.

Another set of proverbs focused on *omenie* which in Romanian means being kind or good, someone showing compassion and hospitality. *Omenie* is what guides behaviour around these parts.

A kind person is only afraid of shame.

An honest woman is the jewel of the house.

Don't walk alone as you will slip and nobody will be there to lift you up.

I encourage you to ask your host about some of their superstitions and beliefs, each family invokes certain ones more than others and most of the time they will do it without realising.

ACI EU MĂ ODIHNESC
POP MĂRIE MĂ NUMESC
FOSTAM ȘI EU AORECUI
FATA BĂRBEȘTEANULUI
STAU LA MASĂ ȘI CITESC
BIBLIA O RĂSFOIESC
CAM FOST FATĂ DE DIAC
ȘI BINE M AM MĂRITAT
LA OAMENI INTIE N SAT
DUHNEZEU MIO AJUTAT
FRUHOSI COPII EL MIO DAT
ȘI DE EI M AM BUCURAT
PATRU FETE Ș UN FECIOR
CE MIOR DUCE AL HEU DOR

CÂT AM FOST PE LUME VIE
MARIE LUI TOADER MI-O ZIS
MIE. ORICE PRASNIC II FRU-
MOS DAR NASTEREA LUI
HRISTOS ATUNCI MAI MULT
ÎMI PLĂCEA CÂND COPII CO-
LINDAU ŞI TU DARURI LE-O
PĂRTEAI. A DOUA ZI DE CRĂ
CIUN CÂND O FOST RÂNDU
MAI BUN ÎN ÎNGER TU-AI SBO
RIT LA PAT SĂRBĂTORILE TI
AU TERMINAT ŞI TE DUGI
LA ALTĂU BĂRBAT DE 10
ANI ÎMPLINEAI. FRUMOS A
FOST ANU CU TRAI 12 NI
ANU 1975 - 2007.

The Farmhouse

Local architecture was influenced by the foreign rulers and various other cultures that have crossed this territory. Transylvanian towns display buildings that have a mix of Romanesque, Gothic, Neo-Gothic, Renaissance, Baroque and Byzantine elements.

Villages are scattered across the vast landscape, with houses that tend to lie close together along the main roads or alongside riverbeds. The territory markings from the Middle Ages generally followed river lines. One such crossing point lies just outside my Mum's village in Manastireni, marking the 16th century crossing from the Voivodeship of Transylvania into the Kingdom of Hungary. Some border markings are still visible if you look closely or if you ask the elders; they can follow streams that have long dried up or simply be buried boulders in corners of plots.

Vernacular architecture is quite similar across Transylvania, however it underwent a marked change after the second World War when more modern construction materials began to be used, such as bricks. Farmhouses are generally small, usually with a foundation of stone and the rest built of wood beams and cob - a mixture of sandy soil, clay, water and straw. Cob is very durable, eco-friendly and doesn't need extra insulation. As the houses are slightly raised, they have cellars underneath and a porch above. There are usually two rooms – one for everyday living, cooking, and sleeping, and a second one, the clean room, for guests, and to show off a marriage dowry.

Roofs are made of straw or wood shingles. Shingles are more popular in the mountains where grains and straw are not so widely available. The barn occupies a central place on the farm, housing the tools, the cart, the hay, the grains. The animals live in the stable which is most often attached to the barn.

Larger farms might have a separate smokehouse, a tool room or a carpentry workshop. My paternal grandfather loved carpentry and was always creating or repairing tools in his workshop.

On the porch of the main house you will often see flowers and plants as decoration. Fruit trees line up the yard and provide much needed shade especially in summer.

Inside the house, the rooms have low ceilings to trap the heat. The layout is dictated by tradition. The bed is placed on the opposite wall to the door, in the most visible position, which exhibits the heavily decorated pillows and blankets. Additional home-made textiles adorn the walls. A bench and a table are on the wall perpendicular to the door; the cupboard opposite the bench, and a stove in between the two rooms to keep both warm. The baby cot is placed in a warm spot, generally between the stove and the bed.

The dowry chest displayed in the clean room is usually the most heavily decorated item in the house, despite the rest of the furniture being simple. On the eastern wall of the house you will see icons; farmers tend to own the ones painted on glass. The local artists include folklore elements and colours specific to each region. There are carpets on the floor, blankets on the walls and bed spreads; they are made of wool if the region has sheep. These home textiles, with their rich palette and geometrical motifs, give texture and vibrancy to the Transylvanian farmhouse.

Traditional artisan items can become objects of desire in contemporary settings as well. Yes, at their core, they are simple, practical, durable, born out of the need to solve a problem. The pursuit of beauty and craft should not be mutually exclusive. Design and craft communities can work together to inspire each other in the creation of collectible items that preserve the essence of the original and bring it into the present at the same time. It would also give the space a fresh identity if we blend narrative elements from one's travels around the world with contemporary finishings.

I can easily picture a traditional pillow or ceramic from Transylvania in a modern minimalist Berlin flat, an elegant salon parisien or a Californian lounge of grand proportions and sublime light. Moreover, what's to stop a classic London townhouse or bold, contemporary Milan pied-a-terre from treasuring a carefully curated collection of folklore home furnishings in a modern yet nostalgic, relaxed chic look. It would create continuity, give energy, spark a conversation, inspire new adventures.

Luxury today is being redefined by time well spent, slowing down, learning new skills, being content, upcycling. I would add to this protecting heritage, ensuring the continuity of traditional crafts by bringing them into the present in eclectic ways, and pairing them with the interests and aspirations of the new owner. There's a lot that can be done when we look to create a thread between the past and the future.

Ceremonies by Season

Winter

FIELD WORK COMES to a relative standstill in winter. The animals keep warm in the stables, the horses are only taken out to collect additional firewood or hay or to spread manure on the land that will be ploughed in spring.

The opposite happens inside the house, where everything gets much busier. Families turn to static activities like picking walnuts out of their shells to be sold at the market or taking corn off the cob to feed pigs and chickens throughout the year, as a supplement to their regular feed. Others weave or knit or embroider; there's enough work to keep families busy all winter.

Throughout December and until Epiphany on the 6th of January, there are various rituals bringing the community together, stemming from agricultural mythology and superstitions. You might encounter groups of masked men in the streets doing various dances or chants, wearing bear and goat masks to frighten off the evil spirits. These costumes are linked to the belief that the dead will return among the living. The goat is a symbol of reproduction and the bear of being reborn; both animals have the power to protect the community from bad omens.

Pigs are slaughtered one week before Christmas, so families have a plentiful table of specialties from sausages to stews, and various cold meat platters. This is an example of a pagan tradition blending with a religious one, St Ignatius on the 20th December. It is believed that if you see blood on this day you will not be ill. Another superstition is that you can only work on this day if you sacrifice an animal. Singing Christmas carols and going from house to house is still quite widespread in Transylvania and a popular way to reconnect with friends and family at this time of year.

On New Year's Day, the tradition is for boys and young men to cross the village with heavily decorated sticks, wishing people a prosperous New Year while singing age-old songs. The ritual is called *Plugusorul* and *Sorcova*. They decorate these sticks themselves and add colourful bows, bells and any other accessory that might make them stand out.

The end of the winter rituals is marked by Epiphany on the 6th January, followed by St John's Day on the 7th January. During the first week of January and as a celebration of Jesus Christ's baptism in the river Jordan, the village priest walks from house to house and blesses homes, animals, families by splashing holy water on them. This way they are protected from evil spirits in the season and year to come.

Spring

THE OLD ROMAN calendar set the start of spring on the 1st March, but the folk calendar celebrates the beginning of the agricultural year on the 9th March. The Orthodox Church decided to adopt this latter date as well for the forty saints' celebration. Around these dates, farmers set their fields on fire, burning twigs and hay stubble to prepare the land for ploughing.

Historically, each village celebrates the first man to go out ploughing. They take him to the river to be symbolically splashed with water before he begins his work.

One of the more joyful, but also one of the oldest spring celebrations is called *Martisor*. You will see women wearing small brooches with intertwined white and red thread. Tradition says that on the 1st of March men should offer one to the women in their lives. It's quite commercial nowadays so you will find them sold in shops and on street corners.

Some theories claim the origin to be in Roman times, when the 1st of March was the first day of the year, and there were celebrations for Mars, the God of War, as well as nature and agriculture. Others say that Dacians wore small stones around their necks, painted in white and red. Red stood for blood, sun and the life of a woman. White stood for a man's wisdom and clear rivers. They would be worn like amulets, and couples would tie them to blooming trees. They signified rebirth and well wishes for the new season.

There are seven weeks of lent before Easter when no meat, dairy or eggs are consumed. No weddings are held in this period either. Every Saturday during lent is also when the dead are remembered and their life celebrated. People are encouraged to forgive those they are upset with.

Easter in Transylvania is a three-day celebration. The week before Easter is called the week of sins. Easter week is also called the enlightened week. Extensive preparations take place for all the food that will be served – lamb, *colaci*, *cozonaci*, dyed eggs. The egg is a symbol of creation and fertility; the lamb signifies the annual sacrifice dating back to pre-Christian times.

The last spring ritual is on the 23rd of April for St George. He is believed to open the gates of the skies for good weather to come and he is also the protector of sheep. This date marks the beginning of the sheep season, when sheep and other animals can be taken to pasture.

Other rituals around this date include splashing water from a river or a fountain onto single girls to bring them a good husband. In my Dad's village, people would attach a hazelnut twig to their main gate on the 1st of May to signal the end of spring work.

Whatever your productivity level, farmers are expected to finish planting their seeds no later than the 21st of May (also another religious celebration) after which it's believed that whatever you seed is for the birds.

Summer

SUMMER IS A very busy season in the fields – it includes working with hay, harvesting wheat, barley and rye. Villagers take turns to pay for a harvesting machine's time as they cannot afford to own one. My parents reminisce about harvesting wheat with a hand sickle when they were young, but that practice is long gone.

Fifty days after Easter, around the end of May and early June, the Orthodox celebrate Pentecost, or the descent of the Holy Spirit to earth.

You might see pots or plates with floral motifs given out after mass in village churches, along with *colaci* to celebrate the dead. In Durusa this practice was alive until recently.

On the 24th of June, for the celebration of *Sanziene* (the associated religious celebration is the birth of St John), young girls take to the fields to gather flowers and to make head garlands for everyone in the family. Some also throw them on the roof, or others put them under their pillow. They hope to see their future husband in their dreams that night.

In July, when the harvest work finishes, there is a celebration called *Cununa*. People bring a wheatsheaf from the field and walk it around the village while singing and dancing to stimulate the land for a better harvest the following season. It can be worn as a head garland or attached to a stick as a wreath. At crossroads it may be dipped in water to bring rain for the crops. The sheaf is kept in a safe place until the new season, when some of the seeds are mixed up with new ones.

On the 20th of July (also a religious celebration), there is a girls' celebration on Mount Gaina, in the Apuseni Mountains. Historically, it was where single girls would go to find a husband. Nowadays it is an outdoor fete with traditional music and food and a lovely and fun day out.

Autumn

THE 6TH OF AUGUST is considered the first day of autumn. The Dormition of the Mother of God on the 15th of August is a central autumn date. Maria, as the most important religious figure after Jesus Christ, is also a popular name in the countryside. On this day, festive tables are laid, families invite relatives to join their feast and it is a national holiday. Absolutely no housework is done. In some regions it marks the day the sheep return home from transhumance. People also go on pilgrimages to monasteries and pray for health and happiness.

The 14th of September is another important autumn celebration, the Exaltation of the Cross. People believe that Earth shuts down and insects go into hiding places. Women take basil to church to be anointed and then they put it in their homes to protect them from evil spirits and illnesses.

St Demetrius celebrated on the 26th October marks the end of the agricultural cycle for autumn. He protects the harvest and is believed to close the gates of the skies.

There are various other smaller celebrations that are meant to protect people, crops and animals from injury and sickness. As they have been celebrated down through the ages, they have become an integral part of the Transylvanian popular culture. I'm sure you will come across at least one, if not more of these traditions continued or revived throughout the region. All it takes is slowing down and starting a conversation with a local, they will be proud to invite you to their celebrations or give you more information about the local traditions and rituals.

The Trouble With Plums

FRUIT BRANDY HAS been a countryside staple for many years. Should you be invited for a meal in somebody's home, you will inevitably be offered *palinca* (pronounced palinka), the local fruit brandy.

There is an abundance of fruit trees in the region, which is perhaps not surprising given that the land is so fertile. Tax documents dating back to the 1600s mention the production of brandy in Transylvania. The elders will say brandy making is as old as time.

The method has been passed down through the generations. Any fruit qualifies for its production, but most often the locals use plums, apples or pears. The plum variety is the most sought after. The drink is a 100% organic, no yeast, chemicals or fertilisers come near it.

Plum brandy from Maramures County in the north is the most coveted for its quality, strength and purity. The name used in this region is *tuica* (pronounced tzooi'ka) or *horinca* (pronounced horin'ka). My paternal grandparents used to produce over 500 litres of brandy every year, which is over 800 pints. My Dad learned how to make it when he was young, and he continues to do so as a hobby, producing up to 100 litres a year.

During communism it was against the law to produce alcohol at home. The farmers secretly carried on and placed the stills inside sheds or barns, the chimney sticking out being the only thing that might have given them away.

You could most certainly buy it in shops, but I would encourage you to try a home-made version if you are presented the opportunity. Most families will have some, and all of them will boast that theirs is the best! There is no wedding, baptism, anniversary or funeral without a healthy supply of *palinca*. Some families may keep some from the year of birth of their children or grand-children to serve at their baptisms or weddings. But generally *palinca* does not age well, except for the one made from pears.

The older generation also use it as medicine; one shot before a meal is said to improve appetite. It's the go-to remedy for toothaches and stomach aches. Local belief insists that it kills bacteria, which is probably true given its 50-60 per cent purity.

Starting sometime in August and continuing into September, the plums are handpicked in the families' orchards. It is very slow work. In my childhood, it was the hardest task - long days spent bent down picking plums up, one by one, from the grass, being careful not to squish them, or mix them up with leaves or twigs. Fortunately, I could escape to school for five days of the week, leaving my grandparents to it. Every weekend, my parents and I, alongside other relatives, would be expected to do our part.

At plum picking time the men started the day early, shaking the trees with long, thin poles, careful not to break any branches. Then, the women and children would follow through the orchard.

It was a very organised process. We each knew our role and we stuck to it. Grandma and Grandpa set the direction in which we should pick. We worked in pairs to encourage each other, and one person walked behind us, ensuring no plums were left in the grass. Mum cooked lunch for all the workers; a dozen people at a time. Come Monday, sitting in my bench at school, I was hiding my black fingernails.

Grandpa paid me five lei in the old currency for each filled bucket. This was enough for a couple of delicious ice creams made locally. Grandpa was a market seller all his life, so he knew how to keep me motivated. That pocket money, and my parents' encouragement, made me feel like a valued member of the picking team.

Once picked, the fruit was stored in huge mulberry barrels, thought to be best at preserving the fruit aroma. We covered them with plastic sheets so no insects or dirt would get in. They were left to ferment for a month or two, then Grandpa would decide the optimum point of fermentation, and signal the preparation for distillation. He always threw away the top layer of plum pulp that had turned brown. He wanted to get to the reddish pulp below, or, if he was distilling apples or pears, the pulp had to be an even cream colour.

The distillation would happen over several weekends. Villagers shared a basic facility; a copper still housed in a wooden barn, close to a stream, with fresh water available to cool the distillation. Each batch of 100-150 litres of brandy would require thirty-six hours of work. Grandpa and Dad would have to distill in three rounds, because the still's capacity was 400 litres, and our barrels held up to 1500 litres of fruit pulp.

The first stage involved taking the still apart and cleaning it thoroughly with fresh water and no additional cleaning product. Once reassembled, the joints would be sealed with a mix of clay, flour and water that was made on the spot. No air would get in this way. Next, the fruit went into the still. If the pulp was too thick, a bucket of water would be added. A fire was lit using the best firewood, all chopped and dried beforehand. Low heat is required for alcohol to transform into vapour. The vapour is then caught and transformed into liquid, dripping out of a thin pipe. The first litre of spirit was always white and not considered good for consumption, so it was discarded. Only the clear liquid was kept.

About three hours later, our 400 litres of pulp would be reduced to 80 litres of spirit. When finished, Grandpa would throw some spirit over the pulp remnants. If they caught fire and the flame was blue, that meant there was still more alcohol to come out, so they waited for it to drip out of the pipe.

The waste from the distillation process would be dumped in the stream or spread on the ground behind the barn as natural fertiliser for spring. The still would then be cleaned very thoroughly, but with extra care this time, as every piece would be piping hot. The low-level fire wouldn't be put out.

A second round of distillation quickly followed using the next 400 litres of fruit pulp. The traditional method to check the alcohol level was to put the spirit in a shot glass and shake it well. If the bubbles at the top were small and numerous, you had the perfect result. Small bubbles are only visible at 52-53 percent purity. If the bubbles were large, the alcohol level was too high. Under 50 per cent, there were no bubbles. Experience had taught my family how to make the perfect strength brandy.

Towards the end of the distillation process, the men in charge would check the taste. When it became bitter, they stopped. The remaining alcohol was called 'the tail', and was distilled for a third time, to reap as much as possible from that one harvest of plums.

The alcohol fumes in the barn were quite strong, I don't know how the men kept on working for so many hours. Villagers would stop by for a chat while all this process was going on, so much so that it often turned into a massive social event, with people tasting the spirit and giving their unsolicited opinion or lending a hand to clean the still. They would tell jokes or sing, and the dogs would be napping by the fire. The women of the family would take turns to supply everyone snacks throughout the day. I loved the community spirit and was happy to shuttle food and plates between the barn and our house.

Two days and three rounds of distillation later, Grandpa would have up to 150 litres of finished brandy from just one barrel of plums. We usually had several barrels to distill, which meant a busy autumn and early winter weekends.

Although beer is now very popular, *palinca* is still the alcohol of choice in the countryside. People drink it alongside *slanina*, bread and onions. The locals do not stand on ceremony when it comes to its presentation. It is gifted to friends and family in unassuming plastic bottles, and everyone smiles as they receive it as if to signal they are in on the secret. As I was growing up, we would also offer it to foreigners, teachers, doctors and any acquaintances in other cities.

Home production has slowed nowadays because fruit supply is not dependable. There are several reasons for this change – the weather pattern shows a lot more variety nowadays, the trees are quite old and new ones are not planted as

widely, fruit pickers are hard to come by. The elders who form the majority of the village population find this work too strenuous for their age. Some of the more famous commercial distilleries in Transylvania today are Zetea in Satu Mare county, and Aciu Palinca de Zalau. You can find these brands in shops and buy some as a souvenir.

In some villages you will also find home-made table wine. It is by no means a sophisticated one, but enough to offer an alternative to *palinca*. Usually made with local, aromatic grapes, this wine doesn't age well, so it is consumed fairly soon after bottling.

By contrast, Transylvanian commercial wine production is an important resource in the region for thousands of years. There are thousands of hectares of vineyards in Transylvania - the most prolific are found in the centre, the southwest and northwest. Some Romanian brands of the past have recently been subject to fresh investment, also new brands have appeared.

Transylvania has its own wine guide, compiled by the prestigious French wine guide publishers, Millau. The first edition was released in 2019, recognising the renewed relevance of Transylvania as a wine region. Some of my favourite new generation wines are: Nachbil, Fetei, Liliac, Wine Princess, Balla Geza and Halewood. The grape varieties grown are: Feteasca Alba, Feteasca Regala, Sauvignon Blanc, Chardonnay, Muscat Ottonel and Italian Riesling for whites, and Cabernet Sauvignon, Merlot, Cadarca, Pinot Noir or Feteasca Neagra for reds.

I hope you make time to discover some of these local drinks and remember to say *Noroc* which means Cheers!

Working With Hay

OF ALL THE seasons in Transylvania, summer is my favourite! There's nothing more special than the smell of freshly cut grass, the gentle summer breeze, warm nights, outdoor naps.

With school holidays lasting three months, there was plenty of time to enjoy glorious summers on the farm. For the villagers however, summer was a busy season, packed from dawn until dark with activities on the farm as well as out in the fields. It wasn't labeled as such at the time but my grandparents were most definitely multi tasking, and dividing and conquering. Grandma would wake up at 4am to prepare the food for the pigs, cook us breakfast, boil the morning milk, and pack lunch to take to the fields. Grandpa would milk the cows then release them to pasture at 5am, followed by getting the tools and the cart ready, looking after the horses.

I loved accompanying Grandpa to our fields in the horse-drawn cart, guiding the animals all by myself, with no help from an adult. On the way, Grandpa would inspect the state of his land and the progress of others. Nobody said it out loud, but they were a competitive bunch and neither wanted to fall behind the season's tasks. Work progress was a regular topic of conversation. Villagers were constantly exchanging information from the state of the harvest to the health of the animals, from the weather pattern to the tractor schedule, as there was only one to be shared in the village for more difficult field work.

When working, not much was said, mostly instructions about next steps. We would work as a crew, small or large, doing whatever we could to contribute, deep in our own thoughts, or listening to the sounds around us - birds, crickets, trees swaying in the breeze. The occasional joke or whistle would break the silence but generally we kept to our tasks, careful not to delay those around us.

As much as I was protected from tough duties as a child, I recognised that hay making is back breaking work for adults, it engages every single fibre in your body. On top of it all, we were working in intense heat all day with a break for lunch and a short nap. I have always been a picky eater but not on the days working out in the fields. The appetite was excellent!

Due to the fertile soil and the rich flora, farmers are able to get a second cut of hay by the end of summer, and sometimes even a third. The first round of hay making would start when the grass was a metre high. The second cut could start at half that height. Each round would take a full month of work that would include cutting the grass with a scythe, spreading it to dry, and finally building tall haystacks. This is how we filled our days from June to August, all hands on deck, travelling for miles to get to all the remote parts of the family's land and ensuring we produced enough hay to last the animals all winter.

This manual work was not for the faint hearted, you had to be very strong to cut twenty acres of grass in a day, working from dawn until dusk. It was one of the best paid jobs for workers for hire because few men could sustain such a level of effort. Today, more well-off farmers have the luxury of using mowing machines to lighten the load, but not then. The added challenge is that these fields are not even, trees, bumps and boulders are in the way. It is not ideal terrain for a machine. In Durusa, my grandparents had so much land that they hired teams of six to eight men to help them every season. They came for two to four days at a time and they slept on hay in the barn. These workers travelled long distances, had a reputation of saying very little, and worked relentlessly.

Once the grass was cut, we would spend two to three days spreading it out to help it dry, and turning it two to three times a day. Then we would use a rake to bring it all together and make heaps. The last step was to build a large haystack, and by large, I mean up to a ton (1,000 kg or the equivalent of two horses) of hay. These large stacks could be left out in the field all winter. The hay stayed dry inside, protected from the bad weather. No one made bales, haylage or silage although on a recent trip I have noticed a few in the fields. Sometimes hay was bartered for corn or other grains if the family harvest was not enough to cover the needs of the farm. This was done mostly by word of mouth in the village.

When the communists came to power in 1947, they started nationalising private property. By 1962, sixty percent of Romania's agricultural land was under the management of collective farms. The state took over thirty percent of the land, and only ten percent of farmers were able to keep their property. My Dad's village was one of the lucky ones, falling under the ten percent. They continued to farm their land independently as they had done for generations. In Manastireni the cooperative was very active and demanding. It operated a quota system alongside regulations for planting and harvesting. It also decreed that families were only allowed to keep thirty acres of land around the house for personal use, to plant vegetables and fruit.

Farmers could keep some of their hay production, about a third, but the rest had to be handed over to the local cooperative. My friends and I used to hide at the top of the hay-filled cart so it would weigh more and count as a higher contribution from our family. It was an open secret.

For potatoes, villagers would have to hand over their entire crop, and the cooperative would allocate a share back to them. Each family had to work about ten to fifteen rows of potatoes each year, each row being about a kilometre long!

Funnily enough, for a region so obsessed with amassing land, there was no clear rule as to how it should be passed down through the generations. It would simply be split up among the children or given to those who needed it most. Sometimes there was nothing written down at all. In the 1960s many farmers' children moved to the cities and were no longer interested in maintaining the family farming tradition. The elders often hauled them back for hay making or more intensive field work.

Despite all these activites, summer was not all work. Every Saturday afternoon we would enjoy freshly cooked *placinte* or large doughnuts eaten outside while sitting on old wooden benches, or on the stone steps in the farm courtyard, sharing jokes and stories with friends and family. Sundays were taken up by going to mass and relaxing in the afternoon, then we would start field work all over again on Monday. Working parcel by parcel, summer would draw to an end and the children would go back to school. All that was left was the anticipation of seeing each other during the winter holiday!

Come Sunday

RELIGION PLAYS A vital role in everyday life. To truly understand its importance in the rural community you have to dive deeper into the history of the region. In the absence of institutions protecting Romanians particularly in the Middle Ages, the church emerged as one of the few places that supported the rights of farmers and their struggles for emancipation. Between the middle of the 18th century and the beginning of the 19th century, two bishops were the only representatives of Orthodox Romanians in the Transylvanian Diet, an important judicial and administrative body that ruled the Principality for almost three hundred years while it was under foreign rule.

In modern times, going to church every week, meeting your relatives, neighbours is a ritual in itself and can strengthen the community. Regular attendance is also one way to be recognised as a good Orthodox Christian.

Christianity first reached the territory of Transylvania in the 2nd century, after it was conquered by the Roman Empire. It grew even more popular in the 3rd century after the Romans left. In 1054 the Great Schism saw Western countries pledge allegiance to Rome, and Eastern countries to the Orthodox Church in Constantinople.

Nowadays, the Romanian Orthodox Church is the largest ecclesiastically independent Orthodox Church in the Balkans, run by its own Patriarch. This means it is not subordinate to any other church, although it keeps close links with the other Orthodox churches in the region. It is the church to which the majority of Romanians belong; eighty-six per cent according to the 2011 census. Over sixteen million people are now believed to be Romanian Orthodox out of a total population of twenty million who live in the country. The other religions are Greek Catholic, Roman Catholic, Lutheran, Calvinist, Baptist, Adventist, Pentecostal and Jewish.

In the Orthodox Church there is no single figure that is above all bishops in authority or jurisdiction; they are all equal and form a partnership. The patriarch is an honorary role, he is a bishop himself and presides the meetings of the other bishops but he doesn't make decisions for others.

Orthodox mass is quite long because it is focused on ritual prayers – spreading God's grace on earth through liturgy. There are no musical instruments; people just sing like in ancient times. If the community is big enough, the church sometimes has a choir. You won't find any bibles or printed sheets in a Romanian Orthodox Church; everybody is expected to know the stages of the liturgy, and the lead singer or *cantaret* simply guides the people in recital. The Orthodox don't believe in purgatory. The dead are honoured in various ways throughout the year – their memory kept alive at most services.

Sunday midday is the best time to visit a village and catch a glimpse of everyone leaving the service in their finest attire. The more isolated the community, the more traditional their clothes will be. Costumes are passed down from one generation to the next, especially since the artisans who created them are quickly disappearing. A new set of traditional clothes, very intricately made, can cost more than one thousand euros, which is a fortune for the locals. I was not allowed to play with the Sunday clothes, they were there to be worn to church and we had a different set of clothes for the house and another set for the field or outdoor work.

I remember my Grandma insisting that my Dad couldn't come to Christmas mass one year without a certain lamb skin coat that the other men in the village were wearing. She didn't want others to think we didn't have enough money to satisfy the local custom, even though we did. He had to have it or else he'd better not show up at all. He only ever wore it there, once a year, just for that one winter mass. People are preoccupied with what others will say or think and generally want to conform to the norms. It wasn't the place to encourage eccentricity, rather it was one where people were disciplined about following traditions and customs. You didn't want to be the one frowned upon. Things are certainly a lot more relaxed today when the elders are just grateful their children and grandchildren are coming to visit.

The seats in smaller village churches are pre-assigned and passed down from generation to generation. In the Apuseni Mountains, men sit at the front of the church and women at the back. In Durusa the seating is mixed for men and women, but I wonder if that is because the community is also much smaller. People recite and sing the same songs and follow the same rules for as long as they can remember. It's another moment of time standing still.

Nowadays, village churches are filled mostly with the elderly. The young have moved to towns and cities, returning at the weekend or for key religious celebrations like Easter and Christmas.

The priest is aware of everything happening in his village and serves as confidante and advisor for the families in the community. During the first week of January, around Epiphany, he visits every family and blesses their homes for the year ahead. The bond can be quite strong. I still remember very well the priests in both my grandparents' villages; they were a guiding force of the community for over twenty years. They always had time for us, offering kind words, prayers, encouragement and appreciation. And a memory of steel I might add, aware of minute details about every single member of our family!

The first thing you notice about an Orthodox church are its many domes. Once inside they are quite ornate with lots of colour and gold paint, an influence from the Byzantine architecture of the Eastern Roman empire. You enter via the vestibule, and you cross the nave - the middle section - to get to the altar, which is hidden by an iconostas, a tall wall covered with icons, with double doors in the middle.

The altar is always to the east and the bell tower to the west. Only men can enter the altar, and this is a very strict rule. Even if you don't see anyone in the church, if you are a woman please don't enter the altar as a sign of respect for the religion.

In the most traditional churches, benches or seating will be available only alongside the walls. It is deemed disrespectful to sit during liturgy; however, you may be seated during the sermon. Not all churches follow this rule today, it's best to look around and follow others.

I have to mention the beautiful wooden churches of Maramures, built in the Transylvanian Gothic style. Eight of these are now UNESCO heritage sites; their towers, up to fifty metres high, are quite a sight. The church in Sapanta Perii claims to be the tallest wooden church in the world. Only a handful of men retain the skill of building and restoring them. There is something magical about the age of these churches, the sound of the floorboards under freshly waxed boots, the century old smell and the silence.

Another striking feature of Orthodox churches are the icons and the paintings on the walls and on the cupola. Orthodox icons are typically painted on wood then covered by a metal sheet, leaving just the face visible. Influenced by the West, from the 18th century onwards, icons painted on glass became popular. They are a characteristic of Transylvanian farmhouses.

There is a rich history and elaborate religious symbolism associated with these icons. They depict real people – Jesus Christ, Virgin Mary, the saints – and are the connection between the worshippers and a perceived heavenly reality. Some icons are said to have healing powers, and you will see people lining up to pray in front of them, or to touch them, in the hope they will make their lives better. These healing icons are mostly in Bucharest and in the south of Romania. But in Transylvania the most notable are at Nicula Monastery near Cluj and at Rohia Monastery in Maramures.

Orthodox churches are very ornate, but there is order in what is shown and painted. The central dome will always have a figure of Jesus Christ shown as Pantocrator, reigning over everyone. In the altar you will find Virgin Mary with Jesus Christ in her arms and the archangels. Virgin Mary is considered the facilitator of redemption and sits between the sky and the earth. All around the church you will see scenes from Jesus Christ's life, as well as the life of the saints, apostles and martyrs.

When you enter any farmhouse, you will notice religious paintings or photographs of religious scenes on the walls, even handmade embroideries with religious quotes and scenes. The rule of each household is to have at least one icon, usually on the eastern wall; east being seen as the source of light, of God.

The church bells are a communication channel for the village. The elders know the meaning of every sound – there's a different one to call to prayer, to mark important moments during mass, to announce death or to signal dangers like flood, fire and war.

In some churches, especially at monasteries, you might hear or see the use of *toaca* or semantron to supplement the sound of the bells. This is a sound made from a wooden mallet hitting a wooden board. It is an older tradition than using bells, the latter spreading from the 14th century onwards. They take turns in using either, as if to signify the old and the new.

There are many religious holidays throughout the year, but I will mention here the more important ones. Easter and Christmas are the most attended celebrations, followed by the Epiphany on the 6th January; the Annunciation in March; Palm Sunday, one week before Easter; Ascension, forty days after Easter; Pentecost, fifty days after Easter; Transfiguration of Christ on the 6th of August; The Dormition of the Mother of God on the 15th August; the Exaltation of the cross on the 14th of September and the Day of all Saints on the 1st November or *Luminatia*, the latter being an influence from the Roman Catholic church and it is only celebrated in Transylvanian Orthodox churches.

There are many more celebrations throughout the year, and if you travel during these dates it would be worth stepping into a church on a Sunday to observe the rituals and the people.

No field or housework is done on a Sunday; it is considered a sin. I have debates with my Mum to this day about not turning on the washing machine on Sunday, or at least not until mass is finished. She considers it work and won't let me do it even if she is visiting me in London.

The other important ritual in Transylvania is funerals. These are even more inclusive than weddings, because the entire village takes part. Church bells are rung in a specific way to let the rest of the village know someone has passed away. The family may place coins in the coffin, meant to be used to pay duties in the afterlife, as dictated by age old beliefs and superstitions.

Ahead of the burial, the body lays on display for three days in a clean room at the family home, a lit candle by its side. All the mirrors in the house are covered so the soul doesn't get stuck in them. At the funeral liturgy the priest recites *iertaciuni* which are prayer-like apology notes from the dead to the ones closest to him. The family gives out *colaci* to everyone, and sometimes even plates and tea towels as souvenirs for everyone attending.

Due to its history of having various cultures living together, Romanians, Hungarians, Saxons, each with their different religions, you will encounter churches of many different faiths within minutes of each other, apparently one of the few places (if not the only place) in Europe where this still exists. Mosques however were never part of the landscape as the region was never under direct Ottoman rule.

Culture and religion flourished once the printed press arrived in Sibiu, central Transylvania, in the early part of the 16th century. From there, it quickly reached other cities like Brasov, Cluj, Oradea.

Manastireni, for example, has three churches - two Orthodox ones, where the Romanians go, and one Calvinist church for the Hungarian-speaking community. Despite pressure from the Habsburg empire for a Greek Catholic church in the village, and a designated plot of land where the church would be built, there was never a Catholic church. The locals stayed loyal to the Orthodox ones, even under the threat of persecution.

A few words are worth mentioning about the Hungarian community church in Manastireni. It's the most important architectural monument in the area dating back to the 13th century. Built in a Romanic style, it had various additions in the Gothic, Renaissance and Baroque styles following the Mongol invasion of 1241 that destroyed most of it. One of the oldest documents in this church is a bible from 1660. The southern side of the church showcases a sculpture of a girl feeding two snakes. It is unique in Transylvania and its meaning is believed to predate Christianity. I've witnessed numerous tourists making a stop to learn more about this landmark.

Churches keep their own records of births, deaths and marriages. Up until 1887, when the marriage registrar was formed by the authorities, the church was the only source of making these events official. When my father was tracking his family history for example, he could only get so far using the local council archives. For anything prior to 1887 he had to dive into the village church archives but could only find details as far back as 1858, then he had to supplement with the regional archives of the church.

Orthodoxy was not an officially recognised religion in Transylvania during the Austro-Hungarian Empire, so many of these church documents were destroyed, and the more important ones made their way to Budapest and Vienna. For example, the first mention of Manastireni was in 1332 in the Pope's fees register, there isn't any other mention in official state documents about this village, despite it being a large and bustling community.

During the communist years, from 1947 to 1989, all religious associations were banned. Showing religious affiliation in public life could bring consequences to one's career or public profile. The Greek Catholic religion was outright banned, their churches demolished. Orthodoxy was tolerated but not encouraged. In the post communism era, going to church and practicing religion is free for all. Religion is very much alive, new churches are being built across the country and there is always a religious figure at important local or national political events. There are about 14,000 Orthodox priests in the country today working in about seven to eight thousand churches; it's difficult to keep track of an exact count due to the ongoing construction carried out.

A commonly used greeting in villages is *'Doamne ajuta!'* - God help us! It shows the strength of the belief in God and religion.

A Few Final Thoughts

I WOULD LIKE to invite you to experience a different kind of tourism, out of the way of bustling cities with their museums, trendy coffee shops and busy squares, and on to villages frozen in time, surrounded by majestic landscape, observing the eco-conscious farmers, learning about their philosophies and rich customs, tasting the delicious food. It will inspire you to reflect on the world around you as you experience the last medieval landscape of Europe and to remember this joyous and bucolic time as a unique moment, one filled with a sense of profound humanity and calm.

Forests are central to the Transylanian way of life, they are home to Europe's largest brown bear population with over 6000 living here, over 2500 wolves or around twenty percent of Europe's wolf population, twenty five to thirty species of birds of prey. All this biodiversity points to a living and breathing ecosystem that works, life from small to large is supported by these last remaining virgin forests of Europe. I read recently that oak trees are associated with three hundred insects. The Japanese prescribe forest bathing or shinrin-yoku in recognition of the preventive medicinal powers of forest walks. Safeguarding this environment should be a priority for all of us, particularly with the recent alarm bells of climate change!

With their deep respect for all things religious and land, these communities have a lot to teach us and the generations ahead. The environmentally friendly farming, the value and benefits of clean ingredients and in season cooking, outdoor living, hard work and dedication, focus and relentlessness, no matter the hardships, energy and good humour. These are values I strive to pass on to my daughters as we see our supermarkets filled with food flown in from every single corner of this world, regardless of season, as our city lives revolve around detailed agendas with every minute accounted for, a lack of extensive nature exposure or seeing animals in their natural habitat.

I realise at the same time that this type of small scale, environmentally friendly farming is not profitable at scale. However a new lease of life could come from involving tourists and the local city population to seek fresh and local ingredients, try new activities in the countryside. We don't have to make a choice between traditional and modern. Let's inspire grassroots support for local artisans, let's teach city children about meadows and forests by taking them a few kilometres away from their school and holding outdoor workshops, encourage them to talk to locals, learn about the land, the produce, the animals, the people involved.

Let's bring to life existing village halls with artisans demonstrating their skills, and teaching those from outside the immediate community. Perhaps public policy that encourages this would help accelerate local involvement.

Keats said that 'The poetry of Earth is never dead' and I fully agree. As we enter 2020, there is a renewed nostalgia for the way things were; let's use the occasion to find a practical vision for the countryside and engage with nature and rural communities with benefits for all involved.

Recently called by Financial Times 'the new Tuscany', I find myself even more head over heels with Transylvania and its village communities in particular. Ironically, the less time I spend in nature, the more I value it. I am proud of this heritage and I would love nothing more than to be able to inspire more people to travel there and discover even a small part of what I experienced.

The new tourism frontier is 'rewilding' ourselves, living 'slow', seeking novel experiences, resetting with sound therapy or meditation. What would you say if you could do all that without breaking the bank and meeting a few interesting people along the way? Life in a village is incredibly hard and it's not getting easier, the elders are incapable of continuing the kind of physical hard labour required every season. We need to get the balance right to help perpetuate this beauty, keep these communities alive before it's too late. We can't stop modernity reaching these villages but we can find new and innovative ways to include rural traditions and impart learnings for future generations.

Acknowledgements

WRITING THIS BOOK has been a humbling experience, a story of personal discovery and reconnecting with the traditions and places that were once the epicentre of my life growing up. Along the way I made new connections that shared the passion for Transylvania, the way of life, its beauty and future outlook. Even though later in life I moved to bigger cities in Europe and in the US, I find myself paradoxically taking energy and inspiration from both of these worlds, old and new.

I am grateful for the infinite support of my family, both in London and Romania. This project became a third child in our family, taking three years to come to life. The conversations and calls with my parents Mariana and Ioan Pop and my aunt and uncle Dina and Ioan Zirbo will now need a new focus.

I will treasure the new friendships created with Aura Woodward, her stories from the projects in the region and passion for what the future can bring, and with Gabriel Motica, his great love for the countryside, its traditions, and all the wonderful people at which he points his camera. It was difficult to leave behind so many other wonderful photographs but I hope they will make their way to you in other forms.

Deep gratitude to everyone who provided feedback, encouragement, suggestions, comments, personal stories, travel tips, introductions. Your efforts are not forgotten: Daciana Branea, Magda Stroe, Anne Marie Martin, Ioana Marinca, Michelle Stoodley, Delia Coldea, Francesca Bacigalupo, Nicole Ion, Ana Ciobotaru, Liana Heuberger, Marco Golla, Madalina Mocan, Sarah Yuen, Father Radu Micu. Kevin Moore and Nigel Mitchell of Biddles Books, thank you for your infinite patience and hard work to bring this book to its final stages.

The diverse resources on countryside traditions available at the public libraries in Cluj Napoca and Baia Mare were an unexpected and welcome surprise. Professor Ioan-Aurel Pop, president of the Romanian Academy, writes very eloquently about Transylvania's complex past. I thoroughly enjoyed his work and was inspired to hear him speak about Romania's history at the British Museum. It's great to witness so many famous international publications turning their focus to Transylvania and I hope this will continue.

Let's open the eyes of the world to a region that has so much to offer!